Guidelines

VOL 24 / PART 2   May–August 2008

Edited by **Jeremy Duff and Katharine Dell**

Suggestions for using *Guidelines*

Set aside a regular time and place, if possible, when you can read and pray undisturbed. Before you begin, take time to be still and, if you find it helpful, use the BRF prayer.

In *Guidelines*, the introductory section provides context for the passages or themes to be studied, while the units of comment can be used daily, weekly, or whatever best fits your timetable. You will need a Bible (more than one if you want to compare different translations) as Bible passages are not included. At the end of each week is a 'Guidelines' section, offering further thoughts about, or practical application of what you have been studying.

You may find it helpful to keep a journal to record your thoughts about your study, or to note items for prayer. Another way of using *Guidelines* is to meet with others to discuss the material, either regularly or occasionally.

Occasionally, you may read something in *Guidelines* that you find particularly challenging, even uncomfortable. This is inevitable in a series of notes which draws on a wide spectrum of contributors, and doesn't believe in ducking difficult issues. Indeed, we believe that *Guidelines* readers much prefer thought-provoking material to a bland diet that only confirms what they already think.

If you do disagree with a contributor, you may find it helpful to go through these three steps. First, think about why you feel uncomfortable. Perhaps this is an idea that is new to you, or you are not happy at the way something has been expressed. Or there may be something more substantial—you may feel that the writer is guilty of sweeping generalization, factual error, theological or ethical misjudgment. Second, pray that God would use this disagreement to teach you more about his word and about yourself. Third, think about what you will do as a result of the disagreement. You might resolve to find out more about the issue, or write to the contributor or the editors of *Guidelines*. After all, we aim to be 'doers of the word', not just people who hold opinions about it.

Writers in this issue

Peter Hatton is a Methodist minister, currently serving in Solihull in the West Midlands. His book *The Deep Waters of Counsel: Provocative Contradiction in the Book of Proverbs* is published this year.

Jonathan T. Pennington is Assistant Professor of New Testament Interpretation at Southern Seminary in Louisville, Kentucky, USA. He holds a PhD in New Testament Studies from the University of St Andrews and has published a number of academic works related to biblical studies and the Greek language, including the recent book *Heaven and Earth in the Gospel of Matthew*. Before pursuing PhD studies, he served as an associate pastor in Illinois for five years. He and his wife Tracy are the parents of six young children.

Grace Emmerson was for many years involved in Old Testament teaching in the University of Birmingham and in the Open Theological College. One of her main interests is the teaching of Hebrew and the enthusiasm that this generates for biblical study. She is the author of *Nahum to Malachi* in BRF's *People's Bible Commentary* series.

Steven Croft is currently the Archbishops' Missioner and Team Leader of Fresh Expressions, and lives in Oxford with his wife Ann and four teenage children. He was previously Warden of Cranmer Hall in Durham and, before that, a vicar in his home town of Halifax in West Yorkshire.

Sharon Moughtin-Mumby serves as assistant curate of Walworth St Peter's in the Diocese of Southwark. Previously, she was Old Testament Tutor at Ripon College, Cuddesdon. Her monograph exploring the sexual and marital metaphorical language of the prophetic books is forthcoming.

Jeremy Duff is Director of Lifelong Learning in Liverpool Diocese and Canon at Liverpool Cathedral, as well as being the New Testament Editor for *Guidelines*. His latest book, *Meeting Jesus: Human Responses to a Yearning God*, was published by SPCK in 2006.

Further BRF reading for this issue

For more in-depth coverage of some of the passages in these Bible reading notes, we recommend the following titles:

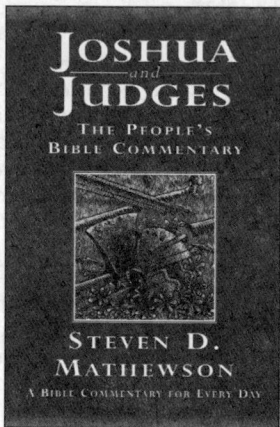

JOSHUA and JUDGES

THE PEOPLE'S BIBLE COMMENTARY

STEVEN D. MATHEWSON

A BIBLE COMMENTARY FOR EVERY DAY

978 1 84101 095 3, £7.99

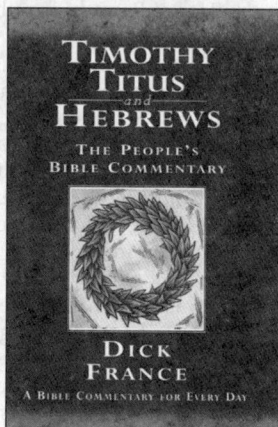

TIMOTHY TITUS and HEBREWS

THE PEOPLE'S BIBLE COMMENTARY

DICK FRANCE

A BIBLE COMMENTARY FOR EVERY DAY

978 1 84101 119 6, £7.99

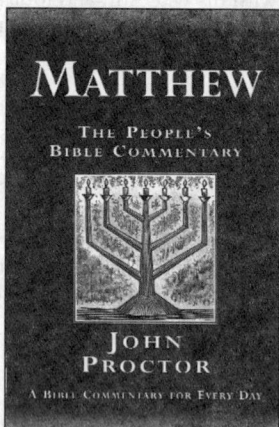

MATTHEW

THE PEOPLE'S BIBLE COMMENTARY

JOHN PROCTOR

A BIBLE COMMENTARY FOR EVERY DAY

978 1 84101 191 2, £8.99

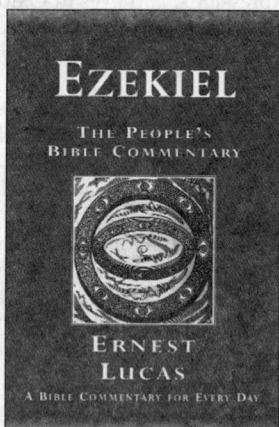

EZEKIEL

THE PEOPLE'S BIBLE COMMENTARY

ERNEST LUCAS

A BIBLE COMMENTARY FOR EVERY DAY

978 1 84101 040 3, £7.99

The Editors write...

This edition of *Guidelines* includes some of the most well-known parts of the Bible as well as some of the most difficult. This expresses our desire for *Guidelines*—to cover the whole Bible, the familiar alongside the neglected, the comforting and the challenging.

We begin with Genesis 37—50, covered for us in this issue by a new contributor, Peter Hatton. This is the Joseph story, well known to many of us through the Andrew Lloyd Webber musical *Joseph and the Amazing Technicolor Dreamcoat*.

This is followed by our first instalment of Matthew, the Gospel for the coming year, which includes the Sermon on the Mount, one of the most familiar and challenging parts of the Bible. Our guide here is Jonathan Pennington from the USA, who has previously led us through the letter of James.

We then move on to Judges 9 to 16, covered by our well-known former Old Testament editor, Grace Emmerson. She draws out the issue of how we cope with some of the more uncomfortable elements in these ancient stories in a modern Christian context. Next are 1 Timothy, 2 Timothy and Titus. These 'pastoral epistles' have their controversial moments as we 'overhear' the conversation between Paul and his associates about how to develop churches. They also contain passages of great wisdom and

warmth and force us to recognize that theological ideas need to be worked out in the complexity of real life. Steven Croft, the Archbishops' Missioner and Team Leader of Fresh Expressions, is ideally placed to handle these texts for us.

After this, we turn to the famous and at times slightly bizarre prophet of the exile, Ezekiel. Sharon Moughtin-Mumby examines highlights from the book and calls Ezekiel 'one of the greatest theologians of the Old Testament'. Finally, Jeremy Duff, our New Testament editor, leads us through the first half of the Acts of the Apostles. This book contains many familiar stories of God's activity and the Church's growth, which give us great encouragement. It also raises questions about the relationships between faith in Jesus and its Jewish 'roots', and challenges us to look again at our own church life and mission. We pray that God will guide you as you wrestle with this edition of *Guidelines*, aiming to be 'doers of the word'.

Katharine Dell, Jeremy Duff

The BRF Prayer

Almighty God,
you have taught us that your word is a lamp for our
feet and a light for our path. Help us, and all who
prayerfully read your word, to deepen our
fellowship with each other through your love. And
in so doing may we come to know you more fully,
love you more truly, and follow more faithfully in
the steps of your son Jesus Christ, who lives and
reigns with you and the Holy Spirit,
one God for evermore. Amen.

JOSEPH AND HIS BROTHERS

People nowadays, it is often said, are biblically illiterate. Certainly, compared with previous ages, those who can quote 'chapter and verse' are thinner on the ground. As a working pastor, however, I am struck by the enthusiasm with which children in junior church react to the Bible, particularly its stories. Communicated in the right ways—ways that remain faithful to the complexities (and sometimes the sheer awfulness) of the situations in which the biblical characters find themselves—these stories are inherently attractive.

This is demonstrably true of the story that we are going to share in the next three weeks—that of Joseph. We shall see him mature from a callow youth to a wise adult, although his wisdom and maturity are gained only through much suffering. His story is inseparable from that of his family, the sons of Jacob, the *benay Israel*, who are also the ancestors of the twelve tribes of God's people. In their story we explore eternally fascinating themes: the dynamics of family relationships, the scapegoating of the innocent and the possibility of virtue even in hard times.

It is significant that this tale has sparked off creative readings by artists and musicians, even in this supposedly secular age. At the level of popular culture, Tim Rice and Andrew Lloyd Webber's *Joseph and the Amazing Technicolor Dreamcoat*, with its engagingly light-hearted parodies of several of the genres of popular music, has been wowing them for almost 40 years. At a more cerebral level, and much darker in tone, Thomas Mann's *Joseph and His Brothers* is one of the greatest novels of the last century—and the longest.

Inevitably, we shall have to select and focus on certain episodes from the 13 chapters in our readings but, if you can find the time, why not sit down and read the whole story at a sitting? You may want to use the version of the Bible you are most comfortable with, but even some of the most respected modern English translations occasionally fail to capture the nature of the Hebrew original, whose language—simple, even homely—is also grand and capable of suggesting huge complexities. The Authorized Version is good at capturing that paradox, but I would particularly recommend a modern rendering—that of the Jewish scholar

Robert Alter, in his translation of Genesis with commentary (see 'Further reading') hereafter cited as 'Alter'.

1 A remarkable family in anyone's book

Genesis 35:9–29

Joseph is a member of a family, the descendants of Abraham. It seems that this family's future, which has been in doubt, is now assured. Certainly the distress caused by the infertility of Abraham and Sarah appears a thing of the past as 'from Jacob's loins' (46:26) spring no less than twelve sons. In them, God's promises of its future greatness (35:11–12) will surely be fulfilled. With the birth of Benjamin, the family is complete. Furthermore, the rivalry between the two branches of the family headed by Esau and Jacob seems to be have been settled as they come together to bury their father, Isaac.

Beneath the surface, darker currents stir. Rachel dies giving birth to the son she names *ben-oni*, meaning either 'son of my vigour' (in which case she is glad that her strength and power will be continued in her child) or, more pathetically, 'son of my sorrow'. Fertility comes at a high cost for Rachel. Perhaps a large family is not necessarily an unmitigated blessing. Significantly, Jacob's name for this, his last son is less problematic. *Binyamin* (English: Benjamin) means either 'son of the right hand' (that is, strong and dexterous) or 'son of days' (that is, of old age). He buries Rachel with all propriety but, strangely, we hear nothing of any grief for the woman he had loved so passionately (29:15–31).

Equally puzzling is Jacob's failure to respond to the outrageous conduct of Reuben (v. 22). Reuben's sex with Bilhah may well be an attempt, as Robert Alter points out, to usurp his father's authority, like Absalom's defilement of David's concubines in 2 Samuel 16 (Alter, p. 198). What feelings must his conduct arouse in Dan and Naphtali, Bilhah's sons? Surely, they must be outraged by their half-brother's behaviour.

This, then, is a dysfunctional family, divided by rivalries and hatreds, headed by a man who seems either unaware of the tensions or so defeated by the task of managing his troubled and potentially violent brood (see ch. 34) that he ignores the problems. Divisions within families and communities are nothing new. The worst thing that can be done with them is to ignore them and hope they will go away. They won't.

2 Joseph—Jacob's favourite son

Genesis 37:1–11

The hidden tensions and rivalries in Jacob's family now surface. Singling out one of the younger and more vulnerable of its members for special treatment is unwise, understandable as it may be in terms of Jacob's psychology (v. 3). Joseph blithely ignores the hatred that this favouritism has engendered, in his eagerness to communicate the dreams that he has been given. Indeed, in his naivety, he imagines that his father will share his excitement at the prospect of his future exaltation over his relatives. Joseph succeeds in uniting his family, but in hatred (for him) rather than love. Ironically, Joseph's dreams will come true. By the end of his story, we shall indeed see his family bowing before him and acknowledging the power and mature wisdom he has gained—but that day is far off.

The ancient world had no concept of the teenager but in this portrait of a self-obsessed and callow youth whose world revolves around himself we might recognize some of the more unlovable traits of that time of life. Tolerance is needed in such circumstances but that is a quality in short supply among the sons of Israel. Marked out by his dress and his claims for himself, Joseph is a nail that they will delight in hammering flat. No wonder his father cannot get 'the matter out of his mind' (v. 11). Jacob has no dreams to warn him of impending trouble (as his son's namesake, the husband of Mary, is to have in Matthew 2:13–15) but perhaps he has some foreboding of the disaster that is to come. Typically, however, he does nothing to prevent it from happening.

How do we deal with the people we find irritating, self-opinionated and 'full of themselves'? Do we seek to discern what is lovable in them? If we challenge them, do we do so gently, seeking to encourage in them a greater maturity and self-understanding?

3 Ordinary men

Genesis 37:12–36

Christopher Browning examines the troubling record of *Ordnungspolizei* Battalion 101, a German unit whose members participated in the shootings and deportations to death camps of some 43,000 Polish Jews in 1942–43. Its 500 members were, for the most part, neither convinced Nazis nor vicious anti-Semites; they were not sadists but ordinary, middle-aged men, many with their own wives and children. Yet, after initial revulsion, most were prepared to kill defenceless civilians, including women and children. How could ordinary people do this?

Browning argues that the explanation lies in group dynamics. A military culture that demanded unquestioning obedience was reinforced by a reluctance to let the rest of the unit down or to leave comrades alone to do what was seen as dirty work—and then the killings became habitual. There was, however, a small minority who refused to take part and, interestingly, were allowed to refuse.

In Genesis 34, Simeon and Levi are shown taking brutal revenge on Shechem for the rape of their sister, Dinah, in the town. So, among the sons of Israel are those who see violence as a way of resolving problems. The others are all too ready to go along, perhaps not wanting to be seen as weak or disloyal, perhaps enjoying the sense of common purpose, noticeable by its absence before.

In our reading, Joseph wanders into the midst of this group, blissfully ignorant of their intentions. Whatever the tensions between them, they close ranks in shared hatred of him, in their willingness to murder him and even to deny him a proper burial (v. 20). With their victim humiliated and dehumanized, they sit down to eat (v. 25), testifying both to their callous disregard for his plight and to the unity they have discovered in their treatment of him. Only Reuben is able to withstand the pressure to conform. His appeals to their greed have some effect, at least in delaying the most extreme solution to their 'problem' (vv. 26–27).

Could violence take hold in the groups of ordinary people of which we are part? When minorities and unpopular people are scapegoated, do we speak out?

4 Poor, poor Joseph?

Genesis 39:1–23

Slavery was a widespread institution in the ancient Near East. Although it was not generally as brutal as the horrific Atlantic trade that carried so many Africans away to lives of brutalizing degradation in the Americas (slaves had some customary rights: see, for instance, those listed in Exodus 21:1–11), it still left its victims at the power and mercy of others. In such circumstances, can someone be upright and virtuous? Can a slave flourish and be successful? The surprising answer given by our story is, 'Yes, if God is with them' (vv. 2, 5, 21, 23).

The narrative is careful not to ascribe Joseph's success simply to his own excellent qualities. True, it is clear that he possesses many virtues: reliability, honesty, diligence and, above all, self-control. In the previous chapter, Judah has shown himself unable to master his lust—ready to give away precious things for a moment of sexual pleasure (38:17–18). Joseph, in contrast, does not misuse his physical attractions (v. 6) but resists temptation and shows gratitude to one who has treated him well (vv. 8–10). However, no amount of goodness and virtue would be able to protect him if God were not with him. Only God's 'steadfast love' (v. 21) —the Hebrew word *chesed* is richly evocative of undeserved loving-kindness—explains the amazing favour he wins with Potiphar, the relative leniency with which he is treated after the false accusations against him, and the success he enjoys even in the royal prison.

We tend to ascribe success in life, particularly success against the odds, to our own pluck, intelligence and hard work. This ignores the fact that such qualities themselves are, to a large extent, gifts—the results of genetic inheritance and being born in a country where people are frequently educated to achieve their potential. Ancient readers were perhaps more aware that many people were trapped in impossible situations from which they could not escape, be they ever so virtuous. They might have been over-inclined to accept such injustices as inevitable.

God's presence with the poor and the oppressed is a judgment both on unwarranted fatalism and self-satisfied belief in our own abilities. Do we count our blessings? Are we aware of God's bias towards the poor and the oppressed? What are we doing to change their lot?

5 Joseph the code breaker

Genesis 40:1–23

In 1861, the German chemist August Kekulé, dozing in front of his fire, had a strange dream of a snake eating its tail. When he awoke, he realized that his dream might offer the answer to the problem he had been grappling with for months—the structure of the benzene molecule. Amazingly, so it proved. Not only did experiments reveal that the benzene molecule behaves in accordance with the model suggested in Kekulé's dream, but the discovery proved to be the key to unlocking a whole new science, that of organic chemistry.

The philosopher of science Michael Polanyi (who, as a research chemist, was himself responsible for many significant discoveries) suggests that reality is like a puzzle to be solved or a code to be broken. Of course, the painstaking, dispassionate, even sceptical enquiry that is central to the scientific method is vital but this enquiry functions, Polanyi argues, to prove or disprove concepts arrived at by more intuitive and imaginative means.

So we should pause before we dismiss Joseph's ability to interpret the puzzling imagery of his fellow prisoners' dreams as primitive mumbo-jumbo. We may be rightly sceptical of fortune telling and the horoscopes in the papers, but in Joseph we see someone who is close to the world of intuition and imagination and who sees faith in God as the key to unlocking the puzzles that we encounter as we live our lives and dream our dreams (v. 8). This ability is combined with a practical approach to life: Joseph's capacities as a household manager and prison administrator are manifest. Both intuitive understanding and practicality are necessary if we are to be wise and lead a flourishing, successful life. Joseph has acquired both, in spite of—or perhaps because of—his experiences of suffering and difficulty.

Yet he is forgotten as the passage closes (v. 23). In Ecclesiastes 9:13–16 we hear of the poor wise man whom no one remembers, but whose wisdom has saved a great city. Perhaps wisdom is a good in itself, even if it gains us no worldly profit.

Have the busyness and pressure of life squeezed out our imagination and intuition? With whom do we share our dreams?

6 Up from the pit

Genesis 41:1–16

Pharaoh's nightmares unsettle him and his land. The first few verses of our passage are liberally sprinkled with Egyptian loan words (Alter, p. 230): 'Nile' (*ye'or*); 'soothsayers' (*chartumim*); 'rushes' (*'achu*). The narrator has taken some pains to produce an atmosphere that his original readers would have recognized as authentically Egyptian. They would have known that the Egyptians saw an intimate connection between the welfare of their country and its ruler. Whatever their precise meaning, the unnatural imagery of these dreams presages a time of upheavals and danger for the land of the Nile, not just Pharaoh.

In such uneasy times, unusual things can occur and unlikely people may be given a hearing. Those who have been forgotten and neglected may be remembered. Indeed, after long years of suffering, Joseph's fortunes take a sudden turn for the better. The language used to describe his liberation deliberately recalls the anguish of his initial degradation and enslavement. In verse 41, he is hurried up not out of 'the prison' (*bet hassohar*) but out of 'the pit' (*bor*)—the same word used to describe the hole into which his brothers flung him in Genesis 37. Just as he was shamed and stripped by his brothers, and by the lustful wife of Potiphar, now he may dress decently and regain his dignity.

Joseph politely rejects Pharaoh's description of him as a soothsayer (v. 15). This is not false modesty but deep conviction. Some versions render verse 16 as 'God will give Pharaoh a favourable answer' (for example, NRSV), but a better translation would be 'It is [only] God who can answer for Pharaoh's well-being (*shalom*)'. Joseph is rejecting the notion that, as von Rad puts it, 'knowledge of the future was open to human art' but he is also testifying to what he has found in his own life. God has been responsible for Joseph's *shalom*, his peace, his well-being —a peace available even in the pit.

When we are at our lowest, how do we discover the 'peace of God that passes understanding' (Philippians 4:7)? What does Christ's rising from the pit mean for our lives and for the life of our society?

Guidelines

Our readings end this week with Joseph poised to make an extraordinary transition from almost-powerless victim to all-powerful administrator, and yet we are only about a third of the way through his story. We probably find it easy to identify with Joseph the victim. We have seen that God has never abandoned him. Will we be able to identify with him in the rest of his story?

Profound questions about power, its use and abuse, are at stake. Joseph's plight was caused in large part by his father's misuse of power—his favouritism and his abdication of responsibility. Most, perhaps all of us have known times when we have been treated unfairly and have been victims of injustice. Many of us, however, are also people of power, actual and potential, in our communities and families. We are listened to and respected. We have influence and patronage. How do we use that power?

Lord Jesus, in your love you emptied yourself and came among us as the servant of all, but you are also the Lord of all. Teach us to use the power you have given us to protect the weak and to restrain the arrogant and greedy. Help us to be brave enough to challenge wickedness and to speak up for those who cannot speak for themselves. Amen

1 Gaining a hearing

Genesis 41:17–36

Is this episode plausible? All we know of ancient Egyptian society suggests that it was socially conservative, a hard place for any outsider to gain a hearing in the corridors of its power. True, there are historical examples of outsiders being ignored until a crisis came: Winston Churchill rose in two years from the backbench wilderness to the highest British office. Churchill, however, was a scion of one of the great ruling families of Britain and had held high office before, while Joseph was an ex-convict from the barbaric (in Egyptian eyes) land of Canaan.

The folkloristic elements in Joseph's tale are clear and should be admitted. They play, perhaps, to the desires of the original Israelite audience to see one of their own getting ahead in the sophisticated, wealthy land in the west. Be that as it may, underneath the naive surface we can detect a profound political and psychological realism. Politically, the food supply was of the highest importance to the stability of Egypt. The extraordinary fertility that made the land the breadbasket of the ancient world was dependent on the annual floods. If the Nile failed to rise, famine would bring with it disorder and revolt, unless measures had been taken to tide over the shortages. Thus, Joseph's interpretations concern the heart of Pharaoh's power. We might speculate that, in this crucial area, suggestions from outsiders as to how problems might be solved were likely to be given respectful attention.

Furthermore, we should note the understanding of psychology that Joseph has gained. He shrewdly manipulates Pharaoh by emphasizing the special link between the king and the divinity (vv. 25, 28): the word he uses is the all-purpose *elohim*, acceptable to monotheists and polytheists alike, rather than YHWH, the specific name of the God of Israel. Not only does this play to Pharaoh's vanity but it also marries well with the Egyptian belief system, without in any way compromising Joseph's own faith commitment.

Implied in all this is God's concern 'lest the land perish' (v.36). How can we as Christians work with those of other faiths, and none, to ensure the welfare of our country and our world?

2 Joseph the provider

Genesis 41:37–57

Is this simply more 'rags to riches' folkloristic wish fulfilment? Certainly, Joseph's sumptuous garments (how often in this story has clothing, or the lack of it, been symbolically important), the emblems of power and its substance, his 'trophy wife' and new name all indicate how far this Hebrew slave has come. However, this social advancement comes at a price. To Joseph/Zaphenath-paneah is entrusted the immense task of planning for a disaster before it has actually happened. As in all such endeavours, he must have been under-resourced and would have had to use all his ingenuity and skills in people management to achieve his goal.

An older generation of scholars saw this passage as an exaltation of the skills of the ancient world's bureaucrats. The extensive wisdom literature of the ancient Near East—of which the wisdom books of the Old Testament (Proverbs, Ecclesiastes and Job) are the Hebrew expression—bore witness, it was claimed, to the existence of a body of essentially secular knowledge, the preserve of a scribal, managerial class. More recent scholarship has drawn attention to the essentially religious nature of all ancient societies; it has noted the importance of particular theological understandings in every national expression of this (admittedly international) wisdom movement. For Israel, wisdom was inextricably bound up with faith in her God: 'the fear of the Lord (YHWH) is the beginning of wisdom' (Proverbs 1:7).

This view is confirmed by the description that Pharaoh and his servants give Joseph as someone in whom God's Spirit dwells (v. 38). The term 'Spirit-filled' is heard a great deal in certain Christian circles, but it refers almost always to someone's spiritual, 'churchy' gifts rather than their skills in the practical spheres of work and life. Should we not also speak of people being 'Spirit-filled' in their daily lives at work and in the home—of 'Spirit-filled' accountants, engineers, sales staff, pensioners or website designers? (Compare Bezalel, the Spirit-filled craftsman in Exodus 31:1–11.)

How conscious are we of God's Holy Spirit at work in our own daily life and work?

3 Payback time

Genesis 42:1–28

Every day, in a building not far from me, thousands of asylum seekers come from all over the West Midlands to queue patiently for their regular report. Most are free to go after processing but some are detained and deported without warning. In the churches we do what we can for them—we have a drop-in centre where tea and sympathy are available—but it is a small thing in the face of such human need. Whatever forces have brought them here—whether economic deprivation, the dangers of war or political repression—they are powerless in the face of a bureaucratic system that decides on their future for, to them, arbitrary and incomprehensible reasons.

It is difficult not to feel sympathy for Joseph's brothers in spite of their past cruelties. The power dynamics have reversed and now they are poor economic migrants at the mercy of a man distanced from them by the armed guards who surround him, the interpreter through whom he speaks and the power of life and death he holds. Moreover, he seems to be playing with them, accusing them of crimes they have not committed, changing his mind over what he requires from them, returning the payment for their provisions. In their bewilderment and fear, they make a connection (ironically justified) between this undeserved ill treatment and the crime for which they do deserve punishment (vv. 21–22).

What, however, of Joseph? Is he not playing the tyrant with his brothers, capitalizing on their powerlessness and ignorance? Can his behaviour be justified?

Once again, we should give credit to the psychological realism of the narrative. Behind the mask of power is a living, breathing, deeply humane man. His changes of plan (compare verse 16 with verse 19) are best explained by confusion at how to handle this extraordinary, unanticipated situation. His repeated demand to have Benjamin brought to him may be prompted by continuing mistrust of his brothers (Alter, p. 242). Has Benjamin met a similar fate to the one Joseph himself endured? The painful memories aroused by the unexpected appearance of his brothers lead him to break down in tears (v. 24).

How can we ensure that the human and the humane are never squeezed out of the systems we devise? Do we pray for those who administer the immigration system in our name, as well as those who are processed through them?

4 Surprise, surprise

Genesis 42:29—43:15

The reaction back in Canaan to the puzzling and disturbing events in Egypt seems, at first, to reveal that little has changed in Jacob's family. Jacob himself seems as self-absorbed as ever (42:36); his extravagant grief over the supposed death of Joseph is now compounded by the unknown fate of Simeon and the threat to Benjamin. Lest we are too hard on him, we should recall what the psychologists tell us about the difficulty of expressing grief in a healthy way when closure is denied—when the body of the loved one is missing or they have been 'disappeared' and their fate is unknown. Be that as it may, Jacob's habit of favouritism, which has contributed so much to the family's problems, is apparently unbroken, even if the object of his special regard has changed from Joseph to Benjamin.

Reuben's bizarre offer of his sons (that is, Jacob's grandsons) as hostages, even sacrificial victims, for Benjamin's safe return is rightly ignored. As a result, however, the painful decision about whether or not to return to Egypt and risk the wrath of the enigmatic high official is postponed until famine forces the family's hand. The fate of Simeon seems irrelevant: they are content to let him face imprisonment alone and abandoned.

We might at first conclude that, if Joseph's demands were intended to find out if his brothers are still the men they were, they have confirmed that selfishness and callous indifference to the suffering of others still control them.

Then, however, something surprising happens. Nothing in Judah's past would lead us to suspect that he would put himself at risk for anything other than his own pleasure. Now (43:8), in order to break the deadlock that prevents the vital return to Egypt, he offers himself as a surety or pledge ('erev) for the life of Benjamin. Offering pledges is a practice that the book of Proverbs frequently warns against (see 6:1–2; 11:15; 17:18) because it places one at great risk, totally dependent on the actions of others, which cannot be predicted or controlled. In chapter 38, Judah had been prepared to pledge his precious signet, the key to his identity, to the disguised Tamar in order to gratify his lust with her. Now he seems ready to pledge his life so that others may live.

Are we ready to believe that people can change?

5 Out of the comfort zone

Genesis 43:16–34

Richard Rohr writes of the importance for spiritual transformation of 'liminal space'—the threshold places (Latin: *limen*, 'threshold') where we move from what we know into new places where we can learn and grow (*Everything Belongs*, p. 47). Liminal places are uncomfortable places. Rohr cites the initiation rites of almost all cultures (other, perhaps, than our own) in which boys move from adolescence to manhood. Often, these youngsters must endure painful experiences (such as circumcision) or nervewracking and disorientating tasks (reading the Torah portion for *bar mitzvah*). Rohr argues that, in an understandable desire to protect our young people from pain, we have unwisely dispensed with such experiences. Indeed, the liminal space is somewhere we all need to go. There we are prompted to let go of the familiar, provoked to change and awakened to cross boundaries into new territories.

Interestingly, 'the men'—as the brothers are described so often in this chapter, perhaps ironically in view of the immaturity of their past behaviour—pause at the entrance to Joseph's house, at the threshold, and express their fears about entering into it (vv. 20–23). Joseph's servant gives them enough reassurance to enable them to enter but we may surmise that they remain nervous. Are they at some level aware of the challenge that awaits them in Joseph's house?

What happens at Joseph's lunch party gives them good reason to remain uncomfortable. There is so much that is strange and discomforting and compounds their existing anxieties: their host's probing personal questions, his unexplained exit and re-entrance, the arrangements for serving food and the special attention given to Benjamin. They are strangers in a strange land, all at sea and unsure of what is going on.

One way to avoid the awakening power of such experiences is to take refuge in drink or drugs, and the brothers are not slow to dull their pain with drink (v. 34). They are, perhaps understandably, reluctant to open themselves to the transformation they need.

When we are next out of our comfort zone, what will we do with the experience? Will we allow its transforming power to work upon us?

6 The sacrifice of Judah

Genesis 44:1–34

It has perhaps been difficult to feel much sympathy for the brothers until this point, even though they have been subjected to much deceit and trickery. 'What goes around comes around' would seem to apply to their predicament. However, the net that Joseph has spread now reaches out to trap the completely innocent Benjamin. It would be easy to see Joseph as vindictive here, toying with those who harmed him, to inflict on them the maximum amount of mental if not physical pain, and unconcerned about 'collateral damage'.

However, we now begin to see how his stratagems might be justified. They appear to have brought at least one of the brothers to the point of a real spiritual transformation. Judah reveals that his pledge to his father to protect Benjamin with his own life was not a tactic to win the old man over but a deep commitment that he is prepared to fulfil. He had connived at Joseph's enslavement and been unmoved by his father's sorrow at the loss of his favourite son. Now, the thought of the enslavement of another brother and his father's grief at a further blow is intolerable to him. He would rather sacrifice himself than let it happen.

It might, of course, be said that Judah's motives remain essentially selfish. He is willing to accept slavery rather than the pain of seeing someone whom he loves suffer. Yet, if he now finds the pain of others more difficult to bear than his own, then Judah is a very different, more sensitive man than the one who was unmoved by Joseph's pleas for mercy. Moreover, we may surmise that he, to some extent, represents all of the brothers. For the original Judean readers of the story, the tribe of Judah was the most prominent of all the tribes of Israel, with Reuben, the firstborn, having long been relegated to a subsidiary role, so it is fitting that Judah should be seen as the moral exemplar, sacrificing himself on behalf of Benjamin.

If Joseph's deception of his brothers is justifiable, it is because it reveals, or even promotes, changes in them that make reconciliation possible. He acts as if in the place of God, using his power and insight to bring about the divine purposes. Do you think it is ever justified to deceive people?

In Dickens' *The Tale of Two Cities*, Sydney Carton redeems his long life of cynicism and vice with one act of self-sacrifice: 'It is a far, far better thing that I do than I have ever done.' Like Carton, Judah shows himself capable of stepping up his moral performance in a remarkable way. Do we believe that others are capable of such advances? What makes it possible for us to change?

Guidelines

Nations and communities look back to their 'founding fathers' (and, more rarely, 'founding mothers')—to the individuals who began the story of the community and, to some extent, determined its character and development. Often such figures are outstanding warriors and administrators (such as Alfred the Great or Robert the Bruce, George Washington or Simon Bolivar) or they are holy people—Gandhi or Mother Teresa, for example. They are often portrayed, especially in popular presentations, as full of virtues with scarcely any faults.

A rather different picture of the founding fathers of Israel is offered in the closing chapters of Genesis. They are shown as generally greedy, lustful and violent men who are often comically ignorant of the truth of their own situations and who lack all self-knowledge. We might recall the rather similar presentation of Jesus' disciples throughout the New Testament. At one level this is profoundly depressing: all of us yearn for heroes and heroines. At another, deeper level it is very hopeful. If God can work his purposes through people such as Judah and his brothers, then perhaps there is a possibility that he can also work in and through us.

Our media dig dirt and leave us with few illusions. Can we still respect those in public life and even seek to emulate what is good in their conduct while realizing that they, like us, are profoundly flawed human beings?

Andrea: 'Unhappy the land that has no heroes!'
Galileo: 'No. Unhappy the land that needs heroes.'
BERTOLT BRECHT, *LIFE OF GALILEO*

1 All is revealed

Genesis 45:1–15

The 'stiff upper lip' is supposed to be characteristic of our island race (although it is a more modern feature than is often believed: Erasmus complained, during his time in early 16th-century England, that his hosts were forever blubbing), so we may be tempted to pass over, almost with embarrassment, the account of Joseph's extravagant outpouring with which this part of the story comes to a climax. We should, however, pay close attention to what his tears express. They bear witness to pain, to a deep sorrow that so much time has been wasted and so much endured by himself, his griefstricken father and his guiltridden brothers. However, this pain is mingled with and overshadowed by great joy. His father is still alive, the wounds of the long years can be healed, and, through all the anguish, God has been working to preserve the lives of his people (vv. 6–8).

Moreover, Joseph's tears reveal the cost to him in personal terms of keeping up the façade of the dispassionate official. The strain of concealing his true identity until he was sure that they were no longer the violent, treacherous men he knew in Canaan has clearly been immense. Judah's willingness to sacrifice himself is the key that opens the floodgates. Finally, Joseph can pour out upon them all that he has been restraining up to now. Movingly, not only do his words imply forgiveness for his brothers, but he also tries to minimize their feelings of guilt and shame (v. 5). Their initial response is, very plausibly, a shocked silence. Only after Joseph has finished can they find words to express anything of the complex feelings that they have (v. 15)

To unveil such deep feelings—von Rad describes Joseph's actions as 'a revelation of himself' (*Genesis: A Commentary*, p. 397)—makes a person profoundly vulnerable. It can be troubling to those who witness it. Not for nothing does Joseph order his servants away to ensure privacy (v. 1).

Christians believe that God has privileged us by revealing, in the cross of Christ, the profound love he has for all humanity (see 1 Corinthians 2:1–7; Ephesians 3:1–6). Emotional honesty and openness belong among those who have been brought into this intimate relationship with God—although, like Joseph, we should know that there are times and places when these things are appropriate and others when they are not.

2 God of old and young

A young Nigerian man living in this country was teased by his workmates about his habit of churchgoing 'with all those old people'. He replied that he was pleased to be with them at worship, for in their long lives they had discovered the reality and goodness of God.

This riposte is worth pondering as the focus of our story shifts back to Jacob. Jacob and another biblical character, David, are virtually unique in ancient literature in being portrayed undergoing the slow transformation from vigorous youth to frail old age (Alter, p. 265). Jacob is indeed physically frail. The news that his son is still alive is almost too much to bear and throws him into some kind of swoon (45:26): Alter points out that the Hebrew *vayyapag libo* means literally 'his heart stopped', and he has to be carried by his sons on his journey (46:5). Yet, in spite of bodily weakness, the old man is spiritually alive and quite indomitable. Once again, he receives visions from God that resemble the more benign of those he had in his youth (28:10–22; compare 32:23–31) and those of his ancestor, Abraham (17:1–8; compare 22:1–19). There is something immensely moving about his readiness to embark on a journey not just to a new land—he has been a nomad all his life, after all—but a new and very different way of life.

In our culture, we often fear old age as a time of inevitable weakness. The biblical witnesses do not ignore the negative aspects of ageing (in 1 Kings 1:1–4, the once virile David lies impotently beside the beautiful young woman Abishag, unable to touch her) but they also speak of the possibility of old age as a time of ripeness and wisdom, respect and honour. 'Grey hair is a crown of glory,' says Proverbs 16:31; 'it is found in the way of righteousness' (my translation).

'The oldest hath borne most: we that are young, / Shall never see so much, nor live so long,' wrote Shakespeare in *King Lear*. How are we dealing with, or preparing for, old age? What are the spiritual resources that we need to be investing in now to help us see it as a time of gifts?

3 An unlooked-for blessing

Genesis 46:28—47:12

There are some textual issues in 47:3–6. The standard Hebrew text has Pharaoh ignoring the brothers' petition and responding by telling Joseph that his family has arrived, although, in 47:1, Joseph has already told him of their coming. The Greek text is more coherent here and many of the English versions follow it.

The main thrust is clear, however. We begin with the joy of the unexpected reunion between Jacob and the son whom he had given up for dead. Ancient Israelite religion had little hope of a full and rich life beyond death: *sheol*, the place of the dead, was a land of shadows where even the praises of the Lord did not resound (Psalm 115:17). Thus, for Jacob, only the fact that his son is still alive makes this reunion possible. Yet those who, in the light of the resurrection of Christ, hope for a time when the shadows flee 'and with the morn those angel faces smile, which I have loved long since, and lost awhile' (John Henry Newman, 1801–90) may see in the account of this meeting something of the joy of resurrection reunions.

Be that as it may, after the tears of joy there is the practical business to be addressed of supporting the family in a new country. Fortunately, the Hebrews have skills in livestock management—an area of expertise that, although necessary, is apparently regarded with disgust by the agrarian, settled society of their hosts. There is little recorded evidence to suggest that such abhorrence was common in Egypt but historically it is clear that Semitic nomads were allowed, perhaps even encouraged, to pasture their flocks in the Nile Delta (of which Goshen was a part). So, in essence, this account reflects the reality of a necessary cooperation between peoples of different skills and abilities. Immigrants brought benefits to their hosts, as many do today.

Yet the positive mood is clouded by Jacob's gloomy assessment of his life and achievements (47:9–10). This should not be dismissed as a 'Victor Meldrew moment'. All the protagonists in this story have suffered so deeply that, even if things appear now to be ending happily, the scars remain. Egypt, moreover, hospitable as it now is, is not the land promised to Abraham and his seed but only another way-station, a land of sojourning.

Yet, in the blessing that Jacob gives to the land's ruler, we may perhaps sense a grateful response for this life he has been offered, with all its complexities.

'For here we have no abiding city, but we seek the city that is to come' (Hebrews 13:14, my translation). Does the notion that this world is a place of sojourning, where no ultimate fulfilment is to be had, fit into our thinking?

4 Desperate times, desperate measures?

Genesis 47:13–31

For the Greeks and the Romans, Egypt was Antiquity—the great, ancient land where civilization began. Indeed, the achievements of that amazing culture over the millennia cannot fail to impress. For over 3000 years, the land of the Pharaohs was generally the most populous and the most powerful political entity in the ancient Near East, maintaining its independent cultural tradition throughout the ages while other ancient empires rose and then fell back into obscurity.

In Egypt's long history, relationships between rulers and ruled were not static. Today's passage, in its description of a time where Pharaoh owned all the land and those who tilled it, accurately portrays what von Rad (p. 411) calls 'the economic absolutism of the state' in the New Kingdom (16th–11th centuries BC). Scholars ascribe the historically attested decline of the free Egyptian peasantry in this period to long-term economic factors rather than a reaction to a one-off event such as a famine. However, we should note that our writer gets the details correct: the 20 per cent tax on farm produce and the exemption of priests (v. 26).

Whatever their cause, these developments are, to our eyes, unattractive, yet they do not seem to be recorded in a critical way. What, moreover, of Joseph's role? Does it not seem perverse that an ex-slave should be the prime mover in the enslavement of an entire people?

We should note that the word *avadim* used in verses 19 and 25 can mean either 'slaves' or 'servants'. It is plain from the text that we are not dealing with any degrading chattel slavery, but something like the nationalization of the most important national asset—the farmland and its workforce—in a time of dire emergency. We might recall the way that the energies of the entire nation had to be mobilized in Britain between 1939 and 1945. The tone of the narrative is, if anything, in awe of the amazing success that Joseph's planning and his shrewdness have achieved. He has been, under God, responsible for keeping alive millions of people in a famine of unprecedented duration.

Can we leave everything to free-market forces in the face of climate change and ecological disaster? Is our civilization likely to be as successful over the long term as ancient Egypt?

5 Weighing up the family

Genesis 49:1–33

The biblical writers were perhaps overfond of lists, in our eyes, but we should resist any temptation to skip them: they are significant both in summarizing previous action and in pointing forward to the future. The poem that comprises today's passage is a case in point. It is full of rare, archaic words and there are textual difficulties. Parts of it may have circulated independently as a paean to the tribes of Israel before being appropriated and adapted to serve as a valedictory on the lips of the dying Jacob.

I was recently on Mount Herzl in Jerusalem as preparations were made to mark Israel's national day. Pride of place was taken by twelve great banners, each bearing one of the symbols of the twelve tribes taken from this passage—for example, the lion of Judah, the hind of Naphtali, the wolf of Benjamin. However, the tone here is more complex than one of simple celebration. It is not just that so many of the images connected with the sons/tribes are negative (for instance, predatory or even poisonous animals) but that Jacob explicitly recalls incidents from the past that are of no credit to some of his sons. At last, he expresses his disgust and shock at Reuben's intercourse with his concubine, Bilhah (v. 4; see 35:22), and at Simeon and Levi's ruthless destruction of Shechem (vv. 5–7; see ch. 34). In the context of the story of Joseph and his brothers, these are hard words for sons to hear from a dying father.

More positive is the prophecy of kingly authority for Judah (vv. 8–10), of a prosperity so complete that he can tether his donkey close to the vines and not care if the animal eats them (v. 11). The scholarly consensus that these chapters—indeed, the whole book of Genesis—received their final shaping in a Judean context is supported by such warm words; they sit well with Judah's role as reformed character and moral exemplar earlier in the story. It is Joseph, however, not Judah, who receives the full paternal blessing (vv. 25–26), even though the tribe of Joseph was one of those lost when the Assyrians destroyed the northern kingdom of Israel (2 Kings 17).

'O wad some Pow'r the giftie gie us / To see oursels as others see us' (Burns). Sometimes the judgments of those who know us seem harsh but they may contain much-needed truth. If God loves us 'warts and all', can we not accept such truth and use it as a catalyst for change?

6 A providence that shapes our ends…

Genesis 50:1–24

The theme of God's providential guidance, which has been implicit in the story so far, now becomes explicit. The actors in the story, for good and ill, have been human (and they bear the responsibility for their actions) but God's intentions have won out in the end—and they have been good, aimed at preserving many lives (v. 20). This understanding of how God works is perhaps similar to that of Romans 8:28: 'all things work together for good for those who love God' (NRSV).

So God's intentions are orientated towards life, but we are left with a paradox. Although we hear of births and new life (vv. 22–23), the end of Genesis is dominated by two funerals. First comes the extravagant set-piece for Jacob, Egyptian in style, even if it is back in the land of the promise (vv. 2–14); then we end with the final picture of Joseph's body in its coffin (v. 26). Do these rites signal completion and an end to the story? Hardly, for Joseph commands that his bones will be taken up and brought back to Canaan (v. 25). Egypt, with its almost obsessive interest in the afterlife and in extravagant funeral rites, has been a place of asylum, but its culture and life are directed towards the past. The future for God's people is not here.

True, that future will be shaped by the past: the internecine quarrels and the violent passions that we have seen among the sons of Israel are not dissimilar to the passions that we will see, writ large, among their descendants, the people of Israel. There will also be those, however, who are wise and close to the Lord, who, like Joseph, will grow to a mature knowledge of God and humanity.

The Joseph option, that of seeking the will of God and never despairing even when times are impossibly difficult, will be one that God's faithful people will discover through national disaster, exile and return.

Our own culture looks back nostalgically so often. How can we lay hold, hopefully, of a future in which God is at work?

Guidelines

The developed world in the 21st century presents a remarkable picture of confidence and insecurity. On the one hand, we are confident in the power of technology to control the world; on the other, we are increasingly concerned that we face problems ahead that we will not be able to solve, while, in the present, many of us experience depression and insecurity. We have immense amounts of information at our fingertips but, increasingly, this makes not for informed decision making but for confusion.

Joseph's story is of someone who moves from an apparently simple pastoral society into a far more complex culture, which is, moreover, under threat from a catastrophic climate change. Interestingly, in his naive and callow youth he fails to understand the emotional dynamics of his family and comes to grief, but as he matures he learns how to thrive in the sophisticated environment of the Egyptian court. He masters a 'wisdom technology' that enables him to navigate through the turbulent floods of the Nile.

As we reflect on Joseph, we are offered an opportunity to increase in wisdom ourselves. Are we in touch with our dreams, our imagination, our intuitions? Are we also prepared to work hard to make our dreams realities? Do we have an understanding of the human heart that enables us to work with others and subordinate our own desires to higher purposes? Above all, do we have the faith in God that revealed to Joseph what the true aim of his life's journey was to be?

Max Weber taught that the most powerful shaper of the modern world was the 'rational technician'—the managerial figure who was immensely capable of harnessing the power of technology but was ignorant of any moral purpose informing that power. Such people will design gas chambers with the same zealous efficiency as operating theatres. We may not be engineers or powerful bureaucrats ourselves, but we commission them and benefit from their skills. The story of Joseph challenges us: to what ends will we use our power? Will we use it, under God, in the Spirit of Christ, to promote human flourishing?

FURTHER READING

Robert Alter, *Genesis: A Translation with Commentary*, Norton, 2004.

Christopher Browning, *Ordinary Men: Reserve Police Battalion 101 and the Final Solution in Poland*, Harper Perennial, 1998.

Thomas Mann, *Joseph and His Brothers* (English translation) Minerva, 1997.

Michael Polanyi, *Personal Knowledge*, Routledge & Kegan Paul, 1951 (out of print).

Richard Rohr, *Everything Belongs*, Crossroad, 2003.

Raymund Schwager, *Must There Be Scapegoats? Violence and Redemption in the Bible*, Herder & Herder, 2000.

Gerhard von Rad, *Genesis: A Commentary*, SCM Press, 1987.

MATTHEW 1—12

It is likely that 99 per cent of everything written and published this year will be forgotten and neglected within only a few years' time. One hundred years from now, most of the remaining one per cent will have been discarded as well. There are very few 'classics' that stand the test of time. The great work called The Gospel According to Matthew is one such rare book. For nearly 2000 years it has stood at the head of the New Testament canon and has been read, cherished, memorized and preached. Monks in France, bishops in Antioch, martyrs in England, Reformers in Scotland, crusaders in Palestine, exiles in Siberia, university students in Illinois, single mothers in Canada, Muslim converts in Indonesia and cannibals in Ecuador—all have looked to this grand book and no sincere seeker has ever gone away empty-handed. The great influence of Matthew on the early Church is still felt today, in that much of our liturgy stems from Matthean language and many of the most famous biblical texts are from the first Gospel, including the Sermon on the Mount and the Great Commission.

The more I have studied this work over the years, the more impressed and excited I have become. The Gospel of Matthew is not only a bold eyewitness retelling of the Jesus story, but it is also a highly skilled literary piece and a deeply theological reflection on the events involving the Messiah, Jesus. It is no accident that it stands as the gateway into the New Testament and as the fulcrum point of the whole Bible. Matthew labours with all his might to paint for us a picture of Jesus as the centre of history and the One in whom all the promises of God have found their consummation.

In these first four weeks of our readings in Matthew, we will venture far into the book. After an extended prologue in the first week (chapters 1—4) we will encounter the majestic Sermon on the Mount, followed by a wide range of stories from Jesus' ministry, including healings, teachings and conflict.

1 Genesis again

Matthew 1:1–17

In light of the high praise that I have just given for Matthew, the book doesn't get off to a very promising start. The first 16 verses give us a concatenation of over 45 names, most of which are only vaguely familiar from the Old Testament. This is followed by verse 17, which seems to make a point out of the repetition of the number 14—not something that seems immediately relevant or profound.

Upon further reflection, however, we can see that in these opening verses of Matthew there is much more than we might initially think. Although it is difficult to see in most English translations, the first two words of Matthew make strong connections between his book and the book of Genesis. In fact, the words translated as 'the book of the genealogy' also mean 'the book of [the] genesis', the very words that are used as the title of the Greek version of Genesis and also occur in Genesis 2:4 and 5:1. This is no accident. This strong allusion to the first book of the Bible serves as a claim that what we are about to read is part of the tradition of God's revelation; the one about whom we are reading, Jesus Christ, is a person of great weight in God's plan. If there is any doubt about this, the following phrases make it abundantly clear to anyone familiar with the Old Testament: this Jesus Christ is the son of David and the son of Abraham. Could there be higher claims made for one's Jewish pedigree? This Jesus is not only a true Jew, coming from the father of the Jews, Abraham, but he is also a son of the greatest Jewish king, David.

What follows is a genealogy showing how Jesus' origins can be traced. Although this seems mundane to us, genealogies play an important part in scripture (and in many cultures today). When we consider the many important genealogies that are found in scripture (such as 1 Chronicles 1—9), we can see again that this introduction serves to connect Matthew with the ancient biblical traditions.

All of this culminates in the summary statement of verse 17. This odd verse gives a superconcentrated history of Israel in light of Jesus' lineage, showing that there are set periods of time between Abraham, David, the exile to Babylon and Jesus. God is in control of all of history. And why is '14' mentioned? This may be because the number 14 is the Hebrew numeric equivalent of the name David. Thus we can see that the text comes full circle, with the mention of David in verse 1 and again in verse 17.

2 Baby king

Matthew 1:18—2:12

In a similar way to the layout of the book of Genesis, Matthew first gives us an overview in verses 1–17 and now he is narrowing down to the specifics about Jesus' origins (compare 2:4–25 with Genesis 1:1—2:3). These first two stories about Jesus are overly familiar to us from the Advent season. It is good to read and ponder them outside of that time of year so that we can see their significance with new eyes. Indeed, the first story about Jesus is both morally scandalous and theologically profound. A less prestigious beginning could not be found: his mother Mary was found to be pregnant before the wedding day and her future husband knew that he was not the father. Despite this, Joseph's righteousness and his heart of mercy are shown in his willingness to divorce her secretly rather than making a public spectacle of her, as he could have done.

Then, a miraculous intervention occurs in the form of a dream and an angel. Yet this is not really the shocking part of the story. The most amazing thing is what the angel says. He does not say that this boy will be a great warrior like Samson or a great leader like David or a great prophet like Isaiah. No, the word from God is that this baby boy will have a specific name, Jesus, which corresponds to his specific role: 'he will save his people from their sins' (1:21). Matthew's comment on this raises the ante even more. Matthew remarks that all of these events happened to fulfil or bring to completion an ancient word from God— that a virgin will bear a son and that his name shall be a sign that God is now with us.

The second story is no less amazing or weighty. Strange visitors from the east come looking for a newborn king in Israel. They do not come in response to an official birth announcement, but because of the appearance of a new star. Logically, they go to the capital of Judea,

Jerusalem, and there they encounter one who does have the title 'king of the Jews' but knows nothing of a newborn king. The notoriously paranoid Herod the Great smells the problem here and sets his mind on one thing—destroying this baby, whoever he is. The significance for us is what this story adds to the previous one. Not only is Jesus the Saviour and even 'God with us', but he is also the King of Israel, as seen by the magi's response to him. Also significant is the fact that the Jewish leaders in Jerusalem are not the ones who go to worship Jesus, but foreigners from the east are. This little observation will prove to be a major point as the book unfolds.

3 A violent beginning

Matthew 2:13–23

Our stories about Jesus' origins continue here and they sadly take a very violent turn. Again by miraculous intervention, the lives of Joseph, Mary and Jesus are spared from the wrath of Herod, but on that day of the slaying of the boys of Bethlehem, many other young parents were not delivered from their grief. This section ends with a final angelic appearance to Joseph, this time telling them to return once again to the land of Israel.

It has been rightly observed that these first two chapters of Matthew, taken together, serve to answer two crucial questions about Jesus' origin: who was he and where was he from? Chapter 1 certainly does focus on the questions of Jesus' descent and origin, hence the long list of names and the introduction of his parents. Unlike chapter 1, chapter 2 focuses on geography. We learn that he was born in Bethlehem to fulfil prophecy (2:6), but we also come to understand why he was later called a Nazarene and why his home base was in Galilee (vv. 22–23). In this way, these first two chapters of Matthew are the prologue to the whole book.

We should also comment on the many 'fulfilment' passages that are found throughout chapters 1 and 2. In our passage for today, we see three examples where the events are explained in light of the fulfilment of some Old Testament prophecy (vv. 15, 18, 23). This continues the pattern begun in the previous stories (1:22–23; 2:5–6). In fact, this series of 'fulfilment quotations' seems to be the organizing rubric in this set of stories about Jesus' origins. The significance is the same as we observed in the first verse of the book. Matthew is at pains to show that all of the many events surrounding Jesus, right from the beginning, are part of God's plan for the world. In fact, they are the fulfilment of all of God's work in the world; Jesus is the fulfilment of the revelation spoken by God through the prophets.

4 A new era

Matthew 3:1–17

Chapters 3 and 4 of Matthew are like chapters 1 and 2 in that they are preparatory: they lead up to the Jesus we know as teacher and healer. With chapter 3, however, we have fast-forwarded nearly 30 years beyond chapter 2. We have heard in the first two chapters that all of the events of Jesus' birth fulfilled the words of the prophets. Now we meet another prophet—a living one—who looks and acts like the mighty Elijah of old. Matthew comments that this prophet is himself a fulfilment of a prophetic word (v. 3), and, if this is not striking enough in itself, his hearers are shocked by his radical message.

First there is the call to repentance. This is nothing new; it is the bread-and-butter message of a prophet. What is new is the reason given for the call: 'for the kingdom of heaven is at hand' (v. 2). This is not just a general call from God to seek him again. This is an urgent appeal of the highest order, based on the imminent reality of a coming event. God's reign over the earth is about to come from heaven to earth. Therefore, now is the time to turn from wickedness and be aligned with him again.

The second part of John's message is even more surprising. When he sees the religious leaders of the day approaching him, instead of upholding them as models or encouraging them as brothers he sharpens his sword even more. While the general populace gets the radical message of repentance, John turns on the Pharisees and Sadducees with words that cut to their very identity. Rather than welcoming them to repentance, he chastises them for the very thing they hold most dear—their Jewish identity as children of Abraham. In so doing he makes a radical claim: in this coming kingdom of God, ethnic descent is of no consequence. What matters is a truly repentant heart that results in the fruit of a changed life.

John is no 'crowd-pleaser', but he is also not one to promote himself. He knows his mission and it is to prepare the way for the one mightier who is to follow. Our passage for today ends with the sudden appearance of this one, to be baptized by John. We see in the baptism of Jesus two important notes. First, the theme of fulfilment occurs again. John is reluctant to baptize Jesus but is persuaded by Jesus' words concerning the fulfilment of all righteousness now (v. 15). Second, we have an undeniable claim about Jesus' identity. If the first two chapters were not clear enough, here in verse 17 we see clearly that Jesus is not just another prophet or leader, but he is something else: he is the beloved Son of God.

5 Exodus again

Matthew 4:1–11

In the climactic scene of Jesus' baptism, the Spirit has descended upon him and he has been declared the Son of God. This high point, however, is immediately followed by the unexpected comment that the same Spirit led Jesus into the wilderness for the purpose of a time of testing or temptation. Mark simply records that Jesus was tempted, but Matthew and Luke each tell us that there were three particular temptations. We may observe that these three temptations, taken together, parallel Israel's tests in their 40-year, post-exodus wilderness journey. In the tests of hunger (Exodus 16), putting God to the test (Exodus 17) and bowing down before a false god (Exodus 32), Israel failed miserably.

Jesus, however, during this 40-day trial, successfully resists the devil in each case. His successful endurance of the same trials that Israel faced serves a strong typological purpose: Jesus is shown to be like Israel (even as Israel was called God's son in Hosea 11:1, yet he goes beyond Israel. That is, he succeeds where Israel failed and he completes Israel's calling. We may also observe many other intended parallels in this text between Jesus and the Old Testament. He is like Elijah, who was fed by winged creatures in the wilderness (1 Kings 19:5–8). He is like Moses, who was in the wilderness and then went up on a mountain to receive the Torah (observe that Jesus is about to go up on a mountain to give a new Torah). As the second/last Adam (1 Corinthians 15:45), he is a reversal of Adam who was tempted, failed and then driven into the wilderness.

The point of all this is very much what we have heard Matthew telling us already. This Jesus is the fulfilment, consummation and perfection of the grand story of Israel, here particularly focused on the exodus.

There is always the temptation to read into this story a message about how to handle our own temptations (for example, 'quote scripture when tempted'). While principles like this may be extrapolated, jumping to this moral application would miss the more important theological point—that Jesus is the new Israel, the Son of God, who fulfils and succeeds where Israel failed.

6 The beginning of the end

Matthew 4:12–25

Our text for today begins with a couple of seemingly innocuous details: John the Baptist has been arrested and Jesus moves house from Nazareth to Capernaum, on the shore of the Sea of Galilee. These two details are the catalyst for the beginning of Jesus' public ministry and Matthew highlights in them the theological point. Jesus' move from Nazareth (see 2:23) to Capernaum is yet another example of Jesus fulfilling a prophetic word, this time from Isaiah 9:1. Particularly, this prophetic word concerns a topic only hinted at in the Old Testament, but one that becomes a swelling chorus in the New Testament—the promise that God will bring light and life to those who are not his people, the Gentiles. Thus we come full circle, back to Matthew's introductory chapters. From the opening reference to Genesis and Abraham, through the appearance of the magi to John the Baptist's strong reproof concerning Jewish descent, Matthew continually depicts Jesus' ministry as one that includes all peoples. We will see this note become a dominant theme as the story unfolds.

Why does Matthew mention John's arrest (v. 12)? This event marks a turn in the eras. Later in the book (11:7–15), Jesus will refer to John as a great prophet—in fact, as the long-awaited return of Elijah. We have already learned that he was the harbinger of the one to come (3:3). With the enforced end of John's ministry, the way is open for Jesus to begin his—and notice that their pronouncement is the same: 'Repent, for the kingdom of heaven is at hand!' There is an urgency of call because a shift of eras has come: the beginning of the end is here.

What follows in 4:18–25 are the consequences of the beginning of Jesus' ministry. He calls his first disciples and then sets about his twofold ministry—proclaiming the kingdom and healing the sick. The result is not surprising: 'And great crowds followed him' from every region (v. 25).

Guidelines

We've covered a lot of ground in this week's reading. We have gone from the genealogy and birth of Jesus all the way up to the beginning of his ministry. These four chapters in Matthew serve as an extended prologue to the book. Chapters 1 and 2 provide background information about Jesus' origins, while chapters 3 and 4 set up the beginning of his ministry. We are now on the cusp of the great and world-changing events that are to follow.

One day I asked my young daughter to turn to Matthew for our time of Bible reading together. I asked her if she knew where the book of Matthew was. Her delightful response was, 'Yes. It is where the Old and New Testaments meet.' In her mind she was referring to the physical place in our canonical scriptures, but 'from the mouth of babes' came a more profound truth. Matthew has crafted these opening chapters to show us, explicitly and implicitly, that the story of Jesus is both part of the Old Testament story of God and also its fulfilment. Part of the fulfilment is that there is a new, ringing note in God's symphony—that Jesus has come to save all peoples, whether Jew or Gentile. Matthew is indeed the place where the Old and New Testaments meet.

How do these texts apply to our lives? I think the primary application that Matthew would want us to make is simple: embrace Jesus. Embrace Jesus as the Messiah and the consummation of all of God's work in the world. He is not merely a prophet or great teacher. He is 'Emmanuel', God with us, who has come 'to save his people from their sins' (1:21). This is gospel—good news—indeed!

1 The blessed ones

Matthew chapters 5—7 are famously known as Jesus' Sermon on the Mount because of the comment in 5:1 that he went up on a mountainside to teach. What follows in these chapters are some of the most memorable, powerful and influential words ever written. The Sermon has been the single most-quoted and studied portion of scripture throughout Christian history, beginning with the Church Fathers and coming down to our own day. We could fill pages with wonderful quotations about the impact of the Sermon and how it serves as a keystone for Christian life and theology. Not only have books been written on what the Sermon itself says; entire volumes have been produced that discuss the history of what people have said about the Sermon. Our purpose here is simpler and more foundational. We want to ask, what did Jesus mean and what is God saying to me today from these words?

In this first section we encounter probably the most famous portion of the Sermon, the so-called Beatitudes. This odd loan word comes from the Latin translation (*beatus*) of the word that begins each of Jesus' sayings here: 'blessed'. We typically think of this word as referring to our own happiness but, in the biblical context, to be blessed means fundamentally to 'be approved' by or 'find approval' with God. This certainly involves our (ultimate) happiness, but the focus is on being accepted and loved by God.

What does this series of 'blessed' statements teach us? Jesus is painting for us a picture of what marks the life of those who are part of the kingdom of heaven (notice how 'kingdom of heaven' frames verses 3–10), and the painting is rather shocking by any standard. The ones who are part of the kingdom of heaven are not necessarily the successful, self-confident, zealous, always-cheerful ones. No, indeed, the 'blessed' ones' lives are often marked by mourning, meekness, longing, hunger and the humility of showing mercy and making peace. Even more striking, we see in verses 11–12 that those in Christ's kingdom can have a realistic expectation of revilement, persecution and slander.

None of this depiction of the 'blessed' ones is appealing to natural humanity. No advertising agency (or church, for that matter) would use this description to bring home the sale. Yet this picture is the life calling of those who are living now under the reign of God, the reign that is currently in heaven but will come fully on earth on the last day. This is the life calling of the disciples of Jesus, the ones who are to be the salt and light of the world.

2 The heart of the matter

Matthew 5:17–48

The Beatitudes are the opening section of the Sermon, paralleled by the closing section of 7:13–27. Our text for today is the first unit in the central part of the Sermon that spans 5:17—7:12. This central part is framed by Jesus' reference to 'the law' and 'the prophets' (5:17; 7:12), which will prove very important for our understanding of this controversial text in 5:17–48.

Why is this text controversial? Because it sits squarely on the single biggest theological question that the New Testament poses: what is the relationship of the law and the gospel? In these verses, Jesus addresses moral issues straight out of the law (often quoting Deuteronomy) and offers his own reading or interpretation of the law. He does this with the repeated formula, 'You have heard… but I say to you'. Thus, this unit of text is often called the 'Antitheses', emphasizing the 'but' between the law and Jesus. However, as I will suggest in a moment, we are mistaken to read these verses as Jesus' anti-law manifesto.

This is apparent, in the first instance, from the opening verse. Verses 17–19 serve as an important qualifying statement that flies over the rest of the passage. Lest anyone misunderstand Jesus' teaching about the law, he makes it clear that he did not come to abolish the law but to fulfil it. Of course, this word 'fulfil' is not new for us readers of Matthew; it has been a regular theme thus far. Jesus 'fulfils' or consummates all that God was doing from Genesis on. Now we learn that the same is true concerning the Old Testament law and the coming of the kingdom of heaven in Jesus. Jesus is not opposed to the law: in fact, he wants our righteousness to surpass that of even the most meticulous law keepers, the scribes and the Pharisees (v. 20). Nevertheless, a fundamental reality is shifting in our relation to the law because now Jesus is fulfilling it fully.

So what is Jesus teaching in this passage? What we find here is a series of instructions on six major moral issues, broken into two groups—murder, adultery and divorce (connected especially to Deuteronomy), and oaths, retaliation and love (connected especially to Leviticus). In each instance, we find that Jesus does not abolish or overturn the Old Testament's teaching; he does something more profound: he gets at the heart of the matter. With adultery he shows that the heart issue is lust; with murder he shows that the heart issue is anger and hatred; with oath-swearing he shows that the heart issue is integrity of speech, not formulaic words, and so on.

This is where the 'law and the prophets' comes in. Jesus' teaching here is nothing other than what the Old Testament prophets had to say about the law. The prophets called God's people to return to God and his ways with a whole heart. God has never desired that we relate to him in a purely ritualistic or formulaic way. In all our rituals and customs, what God cares most about is our heart-orientation. So, too, in Jesus' teaching. The only major difference now is that the final prophet, the Son of God himself, has come and has initiated the final age of the kingdom of heaven. Thus we are to follow this 'fulfilled' version of the law—the law of Christ.

3 Pleasing humans or God

Matthew 6:1–21

In 5:48 we have the seemingly impossible command, 'Be perfect, therefore, as your heavenly Father is perfect.' The problem here is one of translation. The biblical idea behind this exhortation is not that we be 'perfect' in the sense of 'sinless' but that we be complete, single-minded, heart-unified—people of godly maturity, not wavering or inconsistent or hypocritical. This point was fleshed out with six moral examples in 5:17–48. In today's text, Jesus gives three more examples, this time focusing on three habits of personal piety. In each case, the point is the same: our righteous behaviour must be a matter of the heart, not merely outward appearance. The text also provides yet another way in which our righteousness must surpass that of the scribes and Pharisees—else we will never enter the kingdom of heaven (5:20).

Matthew 6:1–21 is another highly structured section. It consists of three parts, each of which repeats the same phrases over again, while the middle part also contains an excursus giving further instruction on the crucial matter of prayer. Our text begins with a heading that sets out the topic clearly: 'Beware of practising your righteousness before others in order to be noticed by them; otherwise you have no reward with your Father who is in heaven' (6:1). Under this heading Jesus will address three common areas of Jewish and Christian practice—charitable giving, praying and fasting—and for each he makes the point explicit: these good works should not be done with an eye to receiving the praise of others, but instead should be done to please our Father God, who will reward us appropriately. Performing acts of piety for the purpose of pleasing people, not God, is what Jesus labels 'hypocrisy', along with the accompanying threat that such a person will have no reward with the Father in heaven (contrast this with the Beatitudes). The application of this truth to these areas of piety is summed up using a slightly different metaphor in verses 19–21. In all our piety, we should be seeking to lay up treasures with the Father in heaven, not on earth, because earthly treasures will be destroyed but rewards with God will endure for ever. This is again a matter of the heart (v. 21).

Although our space is limited, we cannot fail to mention also the Lord's Prayer nested in the middle of today's text. These time-honoured and beloved words are intentionally situated not only in the middle of 6:1–21 but also in the very middle of the entire Sermon. Their placement here is one of Matthew's clues to their great importance. In this prayer we find a simple yet far-reaching example of what God's people's prayers should emulate. In this prayer—not an insincere, babbling prayer like the type Jesus is condemning—we exalt God as the Holy Father whose reign will come from heaven to earth. This is to be our prayer, that the realities of heaven, where God is honoured and rules, will become the realities on earth.

4 True treasure

Matthew 6:19–34

Yesterday's text closed with 6:19–21, in which Jesus uses the image of treasures on earth versus treasures in heaven to make the point that we should be living for the praise of God, not the praise of human beings. We read these verses again today because they serve a dual purpose. They not only conclude the previous section but they also introduce the following segment. Matthew often uses sayings as a hinge or bridge between two units of teaching.

So what is the new unit (vv. 19–34) about? We learn from the language of treasures in verses 19–21 that Jesus is giving us instructions here about the everyday reality of money, and particularly our tendency to be anxious and hording rather than generous and trusting. The command is clear: be concerned with the things of God (heaven), not earth, because your heart is focused on whatever you are concerned about (v. 21).

This is restated clearly in another way in verse 24: we cannot serve two different masters; our hearts must be dedicated either to 'mammon'/ wealth or to God. It is not immediately clear, however, how the talk of the eye and light and darkness in verses 22–23 relates to this theme. Rather than seeing this as a separate saying, it is important to understand the ancient metaphor at play here. The language about the eye being clear or sound or healthy, versus darkness or evil, is a metaphor related to generosity and kindness. The one with the 'evil eye' (v. 23) is one who is not generous or trusting with his money and heart. This is seen most clearly in Jesus' use of the same language in 20:15, where the workers are accused of being stingy (literally, having an evil eye) for begrudging grace given to others. Thus, verses 19–24 all speak about trusting God in the area of money as a matter of living wholeheartedly for God.

The remaining verses continue this instruction. With great words of encouragement, Jesus describes our heavenly Father's loving care for us. God knows our human tendency to be anxious about the cares of this life; this is entirely natural. However, Jesus shows us by means of example that our Father will gladly and faithfully provide for us, even as he does for the birds and the flowers of this world. This is a matter of faith. We need truly to trust God to provide for all our needs. Not to do so is to be 'of little faith', acting like those who do not know God. Anxious living shows that our treasure, and therefore our heart, is focused merely on earthly things. If we will let God take care of tomorrow, however, then we will be freed up to do the greatest thing: to seek first God's kingdom and his righteousness (v. 33).

5 Wise rulings

Matthew 7:1–12

With this passage we conclude the central section of the Sermon. These verses contain a number of wisdom teachings, much like Proverbs. The first several verses deal with the issue of judging others. In the hands of many today, verse 1 is often used to say that we should never criticize or 'judge' another person for their views or actions. Presumably, because we too are sinners, we are in no position to evaluate or pass judgment of any type on others. Of course, to some degree this is true. Whatever verse 1 means, however, it certainly cannot be taken this far. It is clear through-out Matthew (let alone the rest of the New Testament) that we are often indeed called to evaluate between right and wrong, to say that one action or position is correct and another is not. We've seen it close to hand here in the Sermon, with Jesus' strong words against failures in true righteousness, whether they be in the Pharisees or the Gentiles. Then, just following, Jesus exhorts his followers not to give to dogs what is holy or give pearls to swine (v. 6). Whatever this mysterious verse means, presumably Jesus' disciples need to be able to discern who is in the category of dogs and swine and what is holy or not.

Moving beyond this misunderstanding, we can receive what Jesus is teaching here—and it is a challenging word, no doubt. While at times we can and must discern what is right and wrong, we must beware the hypocritical habit of constantly criticizing and judging others, especially our own brothers and sisters in the faith. Jesus illustrates the danger with the ridiculous example of a plank-eyed person trying to remove a speck from someone else's eye. This is a high demand and one that is very practical as we live together in community. There are always reasons to criticize each other and harbour resentment but such habits are condemned as being both foolish and hypocritical. Moreover, we are warned that we will be judged according to the same standards that we hold for others—a sobering thought.

From these negative instructions we turn to more words of hope (vv. 7–11). We are invited by Jesus to seek the Father in heaven who cares for us and will provide for us as we ask. Jesus' memorable image of a father giving a fish to his son is a source of great encouragement as we face our needs.

This section concludes with the famous 'golden rule', Jesus' pithy principle for relating to others: 'do to others what you would want them to do to you' (v. 12). This insightful and extremely practical teaching serves to conclude not only 7:1–11 but also really the whole of the main part of the Sermon. It is a nice summary of the matters discussed from 5:17, particularly, what it means to be righteous according to the true intent of God's law.

6 All or nothing

Matthew 7:13–29

This final portion of the Sermon serves as a conclusion to the whole. It consists of three related sections, each of which depends on a wisdom metaphor. The first (vv. 13–14) is a general exhortation to enter into the way of the kingdom through the narrow gate. This serves as an appropriate admonition in light of all that Jesus has taught in the Sermon. The way to life or the kingdom is not the easy way, as Jesus has shown in his teaching and his own life, but it is the blessed way: it is the way that is attended by the blessings of the Beatitudes we saw at the beginning.

The second instruction concerns the danger of listening to teaching that contradicts what Jesus has just given. Jesus calls such teachers false prophets, wolves in sheep's clothing (v. 15). How can we know who these wolves are? They are people whose lives ultimately show their hearts: a tree always eventually bears fruit according to its kind, whether good or bad (cf. John the Baptist's words in 3:10). These false prophets may appear to know the Lord but are not truly known by him (v. 23).

The third instruction uses the image of house building. Jesus contrasts the wise and the foolish (compare Proverbs) as those who listen to his words and do them as opposed to those who do not. Again, what Jesus has just taught in the Sermon is the matter to hand. There is both promise and warning in these words. At the final judgment, what matters is listening to the wisdom of Jesus.

Together, these three metaphors are used to communicate one crucial exhortation: 'you must follow me from the heart to enter the kingdom of heaven'. This is Jesus' proclamation of the gospel of the kingdom (4:23), and it is shockingly Jesus-centred! Throughout the Sermon and here as well, Jesus is making audacious claims of authority, namely that he alone is in the position to explain the true will of God. Such claims are indeed audacious, and most of all if they are true! We can see by their response that the crowds understand the significance of this point. They were astonished at the authority of his teaching (vv. 28–29). Like them, we are faced with a forked road. We must either listen to Jesus and build the house of our lives entirely on him or we must turn away. There is no middle way.

Guidelines

I hope that from this week's readings and reflections you have come to see more personally why the Sermon on the Mount is one of the most important sections in all of scripture. It is a heavily concentrated block of instructions about the most crucial matter—how we are to relate to God and enter into the coming kingdom of heaven. Unmistakably, Jesus stands at the very centre of this truth. Throughout the Sermon, Jesus' authority is emphasized, and this theme will continue throughout the Gospel. It is no small matter that Jesus pronounces who is favoured by God (5:1–12), gives his own interpretation of the law (5:17–48), explains the nature of true righteousness (6:1–21) and goes on to suggest that unless we follow him we cannot know God (7:13–29). The application to our lives today is no different than it was to Jesus' first hearers: with a whole heart we must follow him and no one else. All other allegiances and understandings must be subsumed under this one sent from God.

The Sermon is foundational, therefore, to our understanding of Christianity. Yet at the same time there is always the danger of reading the Sermon as if it were a standalone document. In fact, this is quite regularly done, and the Sermon then becomes a series of wisdom teachings from the prophet Jesus, comparable to those of the ancient Greek philosophers or Confucius or Gandhi. With this reading of the Sermon, Matthew (and Jesus) would be rightly appalled. The Sermon cannot be divorced from the story in which it comes to us, the story of the whole gospel, and particularly important is the fact that this story will end with the teacher of the Sermon dying on behalf of us to effect these realities in us. The Sermon matters only because of how the story ends, with the death and resurrection of the teacher himself.

1 Cleansing the unclean

Matthew 8:1–13

We have put chapters 8 and 9 together this week because Matthew clearly intended them to be read together. Even more specifically, Matthew shows us how we are to understand the stories in these two chapters and how they relate to the Sermon on the Mount. Back in 4:23–25 we read a summary statement about Jesus' ministry: he went about Galilee, teaching and preaching the gospel of the kingdom, and healing people's diseases and infirmities. This may not seem particularly striking until we get to the end of chapter 9 and find exactly the same wording again (9:35), demarcating this same twofold ministry of Jesus. The point of this repetition by Matthew is to show us that chapters 5—9 hang together as a unit and are to be read together. Closer reading reveals that, in fact, these chapters present these two aspects of Jesus' ministry precisely. The Sermon (chs. 5—7) gives us Matthew's summary of the proclamation of the gospel of the kingdom, while chapters 8—9 furnish us with a compilation of stories about Jesus' healing ministry. Thus we can see that these five chapters together serve as a wonderful summary of Jesus' ministry, bookended with the summary statements in 4:23 and 9:35.

The first two healing stories are found in 8:1–13. It is, of course, very significant that Jesus has the authority and ability to heal anyone; these miracles speak to the fact that he has been sent by God. Yet other men have been given powers of healing, including Jesus' disciples shortly hereafter (10:1). The greatest significance of these first two healing stories is found in who the recipients were and what Jesus said at the time of their healing.

In the first instance, Jesus compassionately heals one of the most notoriously unclean people, a leper. A leper was considered unclean both physically (because of contagion) and spiritually (being excluded from the temple) and thus was on the fringe of society. Jesus not only shows tender care but, shockingly, he reaches out and touches this poor man, thereby potentially making himself unclean as well. The scourge is reversed, however, and the man is cleansed. He then commands the restored man to go and offer to the priests the appropriate Mosaic sacrifice. This corresponds with Jesus coming to fulfil all righteousness in its time.

The second healing is even more scandalous. In this instance Jesus interacts with and is willing to go into the (unclean) house of a Gentile, even one of the Jews' oppressors, a Roman centurion. Even more unexpected is the pronouncement that Jesus makes upon seeing the man's faith. Jesus proclaims that this centurion has true faith in the God of Israel and that, in the final age, this man (and others like him) will be welcome at the table of the great patriarchs. If this were not shocking enough, Jesus adds the dire warning that at the same time many of the 'sons of the kingdom'—that is, the ethnic Jews—will be cast out and punished.

In these stories we see Jesus' compassion and his power, but, even more, his compassion and power directed towards those 'beyond the pale', welcoming in all sinners and cleansing them wholly.

2 Who is this man?

Matthew 8:14–27

The series of accounts of Jesus' miracles continues in today's passage. Matthew records the story of the healing of Peter's mother-in-law, followed by a general description of scores of healings and exorcisms that Jesus performed. This leads to another of Matthew's famous 'fulfilment quotations', this time quoting from Isaiah 53. Matthew's point here is that these stories about Jesus are not simply power-miracle stories, but that Jesus' ministry must be understood in the context of God's plan of redemption. Jesus is not just another prophet with healing powers (like Elijah or Elisha) but he is the fulfilment of the great vision of Isaiah, the one promised by God.

The next two sections likewise speak to Jesus' identity. In verses 18–22, Jesus seems to rebuff some of his would-be disciples. The main point is the difficulty of following Jesus, something he has already taught in the Sermon, but for our purposes it is interesting to note the title Jesus gives to himself here: 'Son of Man'. This is the first occurrence in Matthew of this very weighty expression. It almost certainly refers to the mysterious son of man figure in Daniel 7 and bespeaks Jesus' messiah-ship. In verses 23–27, we see yet another marvel. Not only does Jesus have authority over diseases and demons, but even nature itself obeys his word. This story significantly 'ups the ante' regarding Jesus' identity. Such a miracle, not performed by Jesus' prayer to the Father, but by his own word, results in the honest question, 'Who, then, is this man?' (v. 27). The clear implied answer is, 'The Christ'.

3 The authority of the Son

Matthew 8:28—9:8

Our two stories for today are probably quite familiar to most readers. In typical Matthean fashion, we are not given a great amount of detail about the participants in the story or the setting, but they are vivid accounts nonetheless. Both stories involve the crossing of water, followed by a miraculous healing.

As a general principle, the most important point in a Gospel story is found in the dialogue. The actions of the story do matter but it is in the dialogue that the storyteller communicates his main concern. This is true in both our stories today.

In the first instance (8:28–34), the story of the demoniacs and the cliff-jumping swine again shows Jesus' miraculous powers, but in the very centre of the story is the key. Here we find the dialogue between the demons and Jesus, and the demons' question is very revealing: 'What do you have to do with us, Son of God? Have you come to torment us before the time?' Herein we find yet another (implicit) claim about Jesus' identity. He is the Son of God (recall 3:17). Additionally, we learn something about a coming future time of judgment.

In the second story (9:1–8), the dialogue in the middle of the narrative likewise serves to extend Matthew's description of Jesus' identity. As readers, we are not surprised by now to see Jesus heal a paralysed man, but there is a new element in this story that may be unexpected. In addition to healing the paralytic, Jesus first pronounces, on the basis of this man's faith, that his sins are forgiven. This results in a reasonable reaction on the part of the scribes in attendance: 'This man is blaspheming' (v. 3). They know that only God can pronounce the forgiveness of sins. Jesus' response to them is very important: the Son of Man has authority to forgive sins (v. 6). If there was any question about what Jesus thought himself to be, it is eliminated now. He is more than a miracle-working prophet: he is the Messiah, the Son of God, who will save his people from their sins (recall 1:21).

4 A messianic bull in a Jewish china shop

Matthew 9:9–17

These two stories continue a growing theme in Matthew: Jesus' conflict with the scribes and Pharisees. We are so accustomed to this conflict that it is hard to appreciate how unexpected it was for all involved. The Jewish people probably did not anticipate that when their Messiah came, the leaders and most 'righteous' of God's people would oppose him. The Gentiles would oppose him (recall Psalm 2), but not the scribes and Pharisees. Yet, this was precisely the case. These moral leaders were shocked because they did not anticipate that their Messiah would come among them in a manner that seemed to tread on their God-fearing traditions and, at points, even on the Law of Moses itself. Their logical conclusion was that this tradition-trampling man must not be their Messiah—but how mistaken they were! Today's two vignettes touch on two of the issues that made the Pharisees suspicious of Jesus.

In verses 9–12 we meet a new disciple, Matthew. It is odd enough that Jesus has called people like fishermen to be disciples, but his calling of a tax collector (an enemy of the people, a Jewish sell-out to the Romans) and his table fellowship with such people push the Pharisees over the edge. Jesus' response to their challenge on this point is both perplexing and important. It is perplexing because, on the surface, he appears to be saying that there are some righteous people who don't need his calling and forgiveness. Yet we know from scripture that this is not the case: 'all have sinned' (Romans 3:12) and are in need of redemption. Rather, the point of Jesus' words about the sick and well (sinners and righteous) is to show the Pharisees that, contrary to their expectations, God does care for and redeem the poor and unclean. This leads to the great importance of Jesus' teaching here. He supports his contention by quoting Hosea 6:6, where the heart of God is revealed. God has always valued a heart of compassion and mercy over a strictly outward religion ('sacrifice' here). The Pharisees, in their sincere desire to uphold the laws of God and the traditions, have turned this truth upside down. For them, the details are more important than the heart and thus they fail to understand Jesus' actions.

The point of the second story is very similar. In this case, the Pharisees' challenge about Jesus' practice of fasting (or lack thereof) is answered with a mysterious reference to the future and now coming messianic age. Again, the Pharisees' preoccupation with the details makes them miss the bigger work of God.

5 Even more

Matthew 9:18–34

These verses provide us with four more stories of Jesus' compassionate and miraculous healing ministry. As we have observed, Matthew has collected several such stories (of which there were undoubtedly many more) and put them together as examples of Jesus' power and heart toward the poor and suffering.

In chapters 8 and 9 we have seen the healing of a paralysed servant, a feverish woman, the demon-possessed and a bedridden lame man. In today's stories we add to this list equally amazing and even greater cures.

The sandwiching of stories in verses 18–26 is found in the same way in Mark and Luke, indicating that these accounts were always associated with each other. The inside story of the healing of a haemorrhaging woman is significant not only because of this woman's ritual impurity but especially because of Jesus' emphasis that it is her faith—in him, clearly—that has 'saved' her. This is meant in the physical sense of healing and, using a play on words, in the spiritual sense as well. The outer-shell story of the raising of the little girl goes beyond any healing we have seen so far. Although Jesus tries to downplay the event as another healing (so as to prevent the crowd-control problems he is facing), it is clear that we have here an example of a pre-resurrection resurrection at the hand of Jesus.

The main point to highlight in our last two healing events comes from the responses of those standing by. On the one hand, the crowds react with the revealing comment, 'We have never seen anything like this in Israel!' (v. 33). Indeed, the healing of the blind and dumb is not only nearly unheard of, but it is a sign of the coming end, the age of the Messiah that the Jews were hoping for. Yet, on the other hand, not all respond this way. We have seen the opposition of the Pharisees through-out and now we glimpse an even deeper level of antagonism. In words that both reveal their hearts and forebode danger for Jesus, we see their skewed interpretation of all these events: 'He casts out demons by the prince of demons' (v. 34).

6 Our compassionate Lord

Matthew 9:35–38

These short verses function in several important ways in our Gospel. As we have observed previously, verse 35 is an intentional repeat of 4:23. These 'bookends' show us that chapters 5—9 in Matthew are to be taken together as the depiction of Jesus' teaching and healing ministry. The 'gospel of the kingdom' consists of both content and action, teaching and acts of mercy.

Throughout these chapters, we have also seen a consistent emphasis on the crowds. In these verses they appear again, with the additional description that they are 'harassed and helpless, like sheep without a shepherd' (v. 36). In the modern West it is difficult to appreciate the plight of the average person in first-century Palestine. 'Crowds', to us, conjures images of the shopping centre at Christmas or the mass of people at a concert, but these crowds around Jesus were, for the most part, much like the throngs of suffering Sudanese or Ethiopians we might see on the news today. They were poor, often sick, living in a political and economic system with little hope, and they had no good and trustworthy leaders. In this dark situation we see the character of Jesus shining. His response is a brokenhearted compassion and love. We have seen his compassion displayed already in his many acts of healing and we have heard him rebuke the Pharisees for their lack of compassion (quoting Hosea 6:6). Now we witness the next stage of Jesus' proclamation of the gospel of the kingdom—the sending out of others. Jesus knows that the work of the kingdom must go forth more broadly than his physical presence can extend. The ministry of proclamation and healing must be multiplied, so he instructs his disciples to pray that God himself would raise up more labourers to go into the fields of need. We will see next week that such a sending out of disciples is precisely what Jesus is about to do.

Guidelines

We need the apostle Paul; we need the book of Revelation; we need James. Right doctrine and practical application are essential to the Christian faith, but our New Testament understanding would be impoverished if we did not also have the Gospels, wherein we get to encounter Jesus face-to-face, as it were. The two chapters in Matthew that we have pondered this week make many explicit and implicit doctrinal claims, particularly about the identity of Jesus, and these are crucial to Matthew's intent. Yet we also get something more. We get to see the heart of Jesus and thereby the heart of God, and what we see is that he really cares. God in Christ is a compassionate, healing God who cares about the outcast and the needy. He is a humble God who associates with the lowly.

This Jesus-illustrated truth is undeniably applicable to our lives today. It is good to be in the lowly place, in the situation of need for God, because that is where he meets us with great compassion. With the Beatitudes as our model, we should seek this week to cultivate attitudes and dispositions not of self-promotion and self-reliance but of brokenness and acknowledgment of our desperate need for God. The kind of faith that says to Jesus, 'I am not worthy for you to come to me, but I believe you are able to do all', is exactly the kind of faith that makes Jesus marvel with joy.

1 Horizontal discipleship

Matthew 10:1–23

Chapter 10 comprises what we may call Matthew's second major discourse. We can see that Matthew has structured his book in such a way that there are five major blocks of teaching throughout, interspersed with other events and instructions. The first major discourse was the Sermon on the Mount (chs. 5—7). Now we come to the second main block of teaching, this one focusing on Jesus' instructions for his disciples as they are sent out.

Although chapter 10 stands apart as a new unit of teaching, it is also closely connected with what we have been reading so far. In chapters 8 and 9 we saw Jesus in action, healing and ministering to a wide variety of people. This section ended with the compassionate Jesus exhorting his disciples to pray for the Lord to send out more labourers into the ripe harvest fields (9:37–38). In chapter 10 Jesus does just this. He sends out his own disciples to do exactly what he has been doing—casting out unclean spirits and healing diseases (v. 1).

Several comments are in order. First, it is worthwhile to ponder the significance of what it means to be a disciple of Jesus. A disciple is a learner, not simply for the purpose of knowledge or even the knowledge of salvation, but for the purpose of doing the same as the master. We see very clearly that the reason Jesus calls disciples is so that they might be with him and learn from him, so that he might send them out to do his work. This is an obvious fact but one that I find myself rarely remembering. Quite often, we think of our Christian faith in very individualistic and 'vertical' terms only: the focus of our Christian faith is often on our relationship 'upward' with God. Without diminishing the importance of this dimension, we must not forget that to be a disciple of Jesus is to be one sent out into this world 'horizontally', following his own model in both teaching and actions. What a wonderful and intimidating calling this can be!

If we read the Gospels closely, we see that a major reason why this discipleship calling can be so intimidating is that it will often create conflict and opposition. As Jesus taught, a disciple is not above his master: 'if they hated me, they will hate you as well' (John 15:18; see Matthew 10:22, 24–25). Despite his compassion, Jesus' ministry brought about much conflict and opposition because he was bold enough to stand for God's truth and ways in the world. His disciples should expect no less. This doesn't seem like very good news!

Indeed, Jesus' instructions in our passage today assume that his disciples will encounter trouble. They are instructed to spread the gospel message and mercy freely, expecting that some will receive them and others will not. We cannot avoid the fact that if we are faithful disciples of Jesus, we will sooner or later come into conflict with others in this world and we may even suffer for it (2 Timothy 3:12). But the word of encouragement is that God will be speaking through us and for us as we follow in his footsteps (vv. 19–20).

2 Warnings and consolations

Matthew 10:24–42

Today we continue to read Jesus' instructions to his disciples as he sent them out. Our text continues and reiterates what we read yesterday. It is worth rehashing the point again: to be a disciple is to be one sent out, who follows in the way of his master. There is no other way. A disciple of Jesus is not defined merely by his or her faith relationship with God but also by being one who lives in the world as Jesus did.

This would be an appealing prospect for all of us if Jesus and the kingdom of God were universally loved and received by the world, but such is not the case. The consistent testimony of the Gospels is that Jesus faced opposition, so it is no surprise to see the same thing occur for his disciples—the Church—in the book of Acts and beyond.

In light of this truth, here Jesus gives us words of both warning and consolation. The warnings are that in the face of the opposition we should not fear people more than we fear God or shrink back from following Christ. These are real temptations. It is hard to find in the Bible more unsettling words than when Jesus warns that if we deny him, he will deny us (v. 33). We may not be fond of such a verse but we must understand the weight of what Jesus is saying: to be in Christ is to be a disciple, and to be a disciple is to follow him, even in the pressure cooker of suffering.

Thankfully, such important and real warnings are not the dominant theme of scripture. The Bible does not picture God as an angry, ever-warning deity, but, rather, as a loving Father who nurtures, cherishes and exhorts his children. The words of consolation and encouragement in our passage today are many. Jesus gives us hope that even when we are wrongly accused and attacked (as Jesus was), we have assurance that eventually the truth will be made known and we will be vindicated by God (v. 26). Even more importantly, right next to the dire warning of verse 33, we hear the life-giving truth that God knows us intimately (even the hairs of our heads are counted) and loves us dearly (vv. 29–31). The great hope of being a disciple of Jesus is that, because he is the true one sent from God, he will confess us before the Father in heaven (v. 32). He will claim us as his own.

3 The kingdom-centred Jesus

Matthew 11:1–19

John the Baptist hasn't made an appearance in Matthew since his fiery and unabashed role at the beginning of Jesus' ministry (3:1–17). We know from 4:12 that John was taken into custody by Herod Antipater (the son of Herod the Great, who had tried to kill the baby Jesus in chapter 2). The reason for his imprisonment was that John had been openly calling Herod an adulterer, because Herod had married his brother's wife (14:3–4). Now, as John languishes in a dark cell, hearing the reports about Jesus' ministry, he seems to be having some sincere doubts about whether he misunderstood who Jesus was. Was Jesus truly the Messiah (v. 3)?

It is fair for us to inquire why the great John the Baptist would be asking such a question. The clear answer seems to be that Jesus' ministry and teaching were not aligned with John's expectations of what the

Messiah was to be and do. We know from John's preaching in chapter 3 that he was a fiery eschatological prophet: he was the first-century version of the sandwich-board-wearing 'end of the world' doomsayer, though he was taken much more seriously than we would take such a one today. John, like most other Jews of his day, was looking for deliverance from Roman imperial oppression and for one who would immediately (and with fire) initiate the kingdom of God on earth. This, of course, was indeed what Jesus was doing, but in an 'inauguration now, fulfilment later' way that surprised everyone. The New Testament is clear that Jesus will indeed come a second time in the very way that John envisioned—with fire and judgment—but Jesus' first coming was instead marked by teaching and actions that were not in tune with John's sermonic repertoire. In response to John's questions, Jesus sums up his ministry as one of healing, restoration and proclamation of good news (v. 5).

Lest the bystanders get the idea that Jesus is rebuking or rejecting John, Jesus turns to the crowd and praises John with very high words indeed (v. 11). Yet at the same time Jesus seems to draw a contrast between John the Baptist and those in the kingdom of heaven. What does all this mean? The answer is to recognize the thoroughgoing kingdom-centredness of Jesus. In these verses Jesus is not putting John down but is instead lifting up God's kingdom. He is explaining to the crowds the crucial role in redemptive history that John has played, but this was a role of preparation, and *now* in Jesus the kingdom has come. The point Jesus is pressing on his hearers (us included) is that now that the kingdom has come, a person's allegiance with this reality is all that matters.

4 Truth in tension

Matthew 11:20–30

Our passage for today consists of two parts that at first seem to be unrelated—a prophetic renunciation (vv. 20–24) and a public prayer (vv. 25–30). Yet we will see that in a very profound way they communicate several truths by the nature of their juxtaposition.

First comes the prophetic renunciation. If part of powerful preaching is penetrating hyperbole, then these are potent words indeed. Yet Jesus is not merely using high and lofty prophetic language here; he is making a very profound theological point. Taking the mantle of an Old Testament-like prophet, Jesus pronounces deadly woes on the many places of his ministry that refused to hear his call. Most shocking about Jesus' words is that he favourably compares the wicked Old Testament cities of Tyre, Sidon and Sodom to the places where he was living and ministering. The point is that rejection of Jesus is the highest form of foolishness and rejection of God, because Jesus is the one clearly sent from God, the one who is even greater than the prophets who spoke in the Old Testament, such as Isaiah, Jeremiah, Ezekiel and Amos.

From these woes Jesus moves seamlessly into a prayer to God (vv. 25–30), yet one that is clearly meant to be overhead by the crowds and contains instructive words to them as well. In these words, Jesus emphasizes the truth that, apart from divine revelation, no one can come to see and understand God. Furthermore, Jesus makes it clear that only those whom the Son chooses will come to know the Father. This prayer ends with a beautiful picture of Jesus as the kind, gentle and humble one who invites all to follow in his good and pleasant way.

These two connected passages are a study in contrasts and they may even seem incompatible. For example, we see human responsibility for sin (vv. 20–24) combined with the teaching that only through divine revelation may anyone believe and repent (vv. 25–27). Also, we experience two very different images of Jesus—as fiery judge and renouncing prophet, followed by a sweet and precious picture of him as gentle and caring. Are these contrasts accidental? Do they reveal a patchwork or even sloppy cut-and-paste job on the part of the Gospel writer? No. These contrasting texts reveal the tension in which the truth exists: both are true. We are responsible for how we respond to Jesus, yet we are utterly dependent on God to reveal himself. Likewise, Jesus is both lion and lamb. As we think about God and Christ, we must let these dual truths remain in tension in our hearts and minds, not denying one in favour of the other.

5 A turning point

When we step back and get a bird's eye view of Matthew, we can see that chapter 12 is a real turning point in the development of the whole story. This chapter contains a number of accounts that show the increasing tension between Jesus and the Jewish leaders of the day. Jesus has already had a number of conflicts with the Pharisees and scribes, but in chapter 12 the situation reaches a breaking point with the Pharisees' resolve that they must destroy him (v. 14)—which, of course, they will do (so they think) at the end of the book. The turning point of chapter 12 is also seen in a shift in Jesus' ministry style, method and focus: in verse 15 he withdraws from a thoroughly open and public ministry to focus on those who want to follow him, and, very significantly, in chapter 13 he begins for the first time to teach in parables. Just as significantly, we learn from 12:17 that Jesus is now fulfilling God's final plan (as prophesied by Isaiah) to bring grace to all peoples. This is good news!

So what is the situation that causes this major turning point? It revolves around one of the single most important elements in Jewish identity, the keeping of the sabbath. It is hard to overestimate how important sabbath keeping was and is to the Jewish people, so when Jesus challenges this core value, we should not be surprised at their violent reaction.

How does Jesus justify his seemingly 'new' and lax view of the sabbath? He does so in a number of ways. First, he shows how the Jews have misunderstood their own tradition and have misplaced their priorities. Contrary to the Pharisees' view, the sabbath is not an ultimate matter of righteousness. The law itself permits its breaking under certain circumstances (vv. 3–5) and there are higher values, such as compassion and care for others (vv. 7–13). A second and subtler way that Jesus grounds his actions is found in verses 6 and 8. In both of these verses, Jesus makes bold claims about himself. He is able to reinterpret the sabbath because 'something greater than the temple is here' and because, as the Son of Man, he is Lord over the sabbath. As we have found time and again in Matthew, the underlying point is emphasized: in Jesus we are dealing with not just a prophet or priest or God-ordained spokesman but one who is greater than all of these—'God with us' in the flesh.

6 'Choose this day...'

As we saw yesterday, this chapter marks a turning point in the whole book. The Pharisees have now decided that Jesus is not the Messiah and must be put to death (12:14). At the same time, Jesus has turned his ministry towards a conscious fulfilment of the gospel to all peoples and a focus only on his followers (12:15–21). It is in this context that we understand the events of today's text.

The Pharisees now make their boldest and sharpest attacks on Jesus. Even as the crowds wonder aloud if Jesus is the Davidic Messiah (v. 23), they accuse him of being demonic. Knowing their thoughts and hearts, Jesus turns on them with searing and undeniable logic: it is an absurd and impossible argument to say that Jesus is casting out demons by the power of demons; such a divided house would only defeat itself! Going on the attack, Jesus calls such an argument the one unpardonable sin (vv. 30–32). Instead, all people must decide: proclaim Jesus either as good or as evil; he cannot be both. Whichever proclamation a person makes shall be the basis of their future judgment (vv. 33–37).

The Pharisees don't stop there, however. Their words dripping with sarcasm, they call him 'Teacher' and facetiously ask him for a sign (v. 38). Once again Jesus knows their hearts and cuts to the quick of the matter. They do not need a sign, although they will be given one at the resurrection of Jesus. What they need is to recognize that one greater than Jonah or Solomon is in their midst. As a result of their rejection of him, great will be their judgment.

Our chapter ends with a radical restatement of one of Jesus' main themes: the people of God are now defined not by ethnicity, super-conscientious religious observance or family background, but by one criterion—identity with the Father in heaven through his Son on earth (v. 50).

I have entitled this section 'Choose this day...' in reference to Joshua's famous call to the people of Israel to decide whether they would follow God or some other way (Joshua 24:15). The same thing is occurring here in Matthew. At this turning point of the whole book, we, along with Jesus' original hearers, face the momentous decision: will we align ourselves with Jesus or not? Will we be Jesus' brothers in the will of God or will we be an evil and adulterous generation? There is no inbetween.

Guidelines

The density and richness of the material in this week's passages has required that we spend more time unpacking the basic meaning than in direct application to our lives. As we conclude this week's readings and reflect upon them, let me offer a few thoughts.

These chapters in Matthew are a call for us to be disciples of Jesus. A view of God's claim on our lives that is mild and mellow misses the radical nature of Jesus' message. Jesus presents himself as a fork in the road. There is no neutral position or attitude towards Jesus. There is no standing still. There is no option to view Jesus as a good man or teacher who demands little of us. A disciple is a follower of the master.

Lest we be discouraged by this high calling, our passages this week are ripe with encouraging fruit: as we follow Jesus, God will provide for our needs; he cares for us richly; he is a gentle and humble master; he will not crush a bruised soul, and he calls us his brothers and sisters.

So what does it mean to be a disciple, following our model, Jesus? It means on the one hand that we publicly stand for truth in a loving way. We see Jesus doing this continually. On the other hand, it means that we privately relate to others in a gentle and humble way, seeking their good, not our own, also modelled by the Lord. This latter truth is hardest to put into practice with those who are closest to us, especially those in our own family. This may be a good place to start this week as we follow Jesus' way.

FURTHER READING

The resources on Matthew are manifold. For commentaries on Matthew, the reader would especially benefit much from the works of R.T. France. His older commentary is in the Tyndale New Testament Commentary series, published by IVP. He has also written a recent commentary in the New International Commentary on the New Testament (NICNT) series, published by Eerdmans. On the Sermon on the Mount in particular, again, there are many excellent books. I particularly like Dale Allison's *The Sermon on the Mount: Inspiring the Moral Imagination* (Crossroad, 1999).

JUDGES 9—16

Judges is part of a longer story. Moses and his successor Joshua are dead. Israel is in the promised land but not yet a unified society in the period 1200–1050BC. In chapters 9—16 we have a series of 'snapshots' of local heroes raised up to meet specific needs in desperate situations.

The name 'judges' is somewhat misleading in modern English. True, among the charismatic figures there are 'minor judges' who acted in a judicial capacity, as indeed Samuel did later (1 Samuel 7:11–17). Theirs seems to have been a lifelong office, briefly recorded in a traditional formula. But for the major figures, whose exploits are told in chapters 9 to 16, the Hebrew word *shophet* signifies a 'deliverer', someone who brought freedom from oppression, not in the context of a law court but on the stage of history. Attempts to reconstruct the period historically are unsatisfactory, but close reading of the text yields rich results in the social customs of the time and in theological understanding. These ancient stories have been set down as a warning to later Israel of the folly of forgetting the past mercies of the Lord and his power to deliver.

Judges is a disturbing, unsettling book for our reading as Christians today. It raises moral as well as theological questions. What kind of God is this who seems to be involved in such brutal actions? Are disaster and suffering always the result of disobedience to the Lord? It is a world far removed from ours in many of its customs and attitudes but not, sadly, in its brutality and nor, as we shall see, in the arrogance of some in their attempts to manipulate God in pursuit of their own aims.

We can read Judges on two levels: delighting in the artistry of the ancient storytellers and / or as holy scripture written also for our learning, despite the questions of an ethical and theological kind that cannot be ignored. Israel in the promised land was struggling for survival against powerful enemies, principally Ammonites to the east and Philistines to the west. Tribal alliances were weak and growing weaker, as can be seen from the song of Deborah in chapter 5 to the final disintegration in civil war at the end of the book.

These notes are based mainly on the New Revised Standard Version.

1 Abimelech

Judges 9:1–25

A new section brings a new judge, Abimelech, but earlier events already cast a shadow. The previous chapter ends on an ominous note of ingratitude to the Lord and disloyalty to Gideon 'in return for all the good that he had done for Israel' (8:35). Gideon's refusal of kingship for himself and his son had been uncompromising: 'the Lord will rule over you' (8:23). Now here is one of Gideon's sons ambitious for power, and he an outsider—the son of a concubine, although Gideon had many wives (8:30–31).

Abimelech has 70 brothers (v. 2). He has other family, too, who owe those brothers no loyalty. A support group, his mother's family, awaits him in Shechem, his birthplace. To them he puts the question: which is preferable, 70 rulers (an expensive proposition) or one? 'And don't forget that I am one of yours,' he adds. The number 70 recurs in verse, this time referring to 70 silver pieces. Abimelech needs resources. Notice where the silver comes from: a temple of Baal-Berith, taken in an act of sacrilege. The narrator has no sympathy for Abimelech. The men he hires with his stolen wealth are no better than a rabble. Abimelech is cold and calculating, slaughtering his half-brothers without mercy 'on one stone' (v. 5, a chilling phrase echoed later in the story).

Abimelech becomes not just leader but 'king' (v. 6), the first to bear that title in ancient Israel. The word is explicit, and the solemnity of the occasion makes the location itself memorable ('the oak of the pillar', an obscure phrase). That is not the end of the story, though. One brother has survived and he, like Gideon, is resolutely opposed to the idea of kingship. From Mount Gerizim (notable in both Old and New Testaments: see Joshua 8:30–35 and John 4:20) Jotham, at risk of his life (v. 21), enunciates a powerful fable, a word from the Lord.

His critique of kingship is devastating. It is a useless diversion from fruitful service. Olive, fig and vine, basic to the community's needs, refuse to abandon their essential role in order to 'sway' (the word is ironical) over others. Only the wild, uncultivated bramble (more at home in thickets) accepts the invitation, offering what it cannot give, namely shelter to trees taller and nobler than itself. It also comes with a destructive threat, to consume even the majestic cedars of Lebanon—a destruction brutally enacted in what is to follow.

2 A curse fulfilled

Judges 9:26–41, 46–57

This is a story of shifting loyalties, of a disintegrating society and finally of fiery destruction—all the result of ruthless, self-serving ambition. Disloyalty was endemic in Shechem: the people show no loyalty to Gideon, their earlier hero (8:35), and now no loyalty to the king they have freely chosen. For Abimelech, no violence was too horrific, no slaughter too brutal to bolster his power. Where in his story is there any hint of commitment to God, the authority beyond all human power? The bramble's threat of destruction by fire (9:15) becomes a grim reality for the lords of Shechem (v. 49). Abimelech, their would-be deliverer, becomes their oppressor until, with superb irony, a quickwitted woman becomes the deliverer, her only weapon a common domestic object. The skull of Abimelech, who killed his 70 brothers 'on one stone', is crushed by a stone. The dying Abimelech is less troubled by death than by the humiliation that he dies at a woman's hand (v. 54), while she, the saviour, remains nameless.

Abimelech's story is more than this. It warns of the dangers of ambitious leadership without commitment to the Lord, and specifically of the dangers of kingship. There are two contrasting strands in Judges: as here, there is a strongly anti-kingship stance (because the Lord is king, 8:23), but in chapters 17—21 we find approval of kingship as the means of stability in a disintegrating society rushing headlong to disaster. It has been suggested that these two contrasting modes of leadership, judges versus monarchy, are an underlying theme of the book, exploring the tension between continuity of leadership providing stability through dynastic kingship on the one hand, and Yahweh's freedom to raise up charismatic leaders in times of emergency on the other.

With dynastic monarchy, where is Yahweh's freedom? One might ask this question in Abimelech's case. Unlike some of his predecessors, who were raised up by God to meet a particular situation (for example, Ehud in 3:15 and Gideon in 6:14), Abimelech seizes power for himself without divine approval. His story illustrates the power of words to stir up anger (vv. 28–29) and the subsequent massive bloodshed and gratuitous slaughter of civilians (vv. 42–45). For the Old Testament writer, all is within God's control and the despicable crime of fratricide is avenged (vv. 24, 56). We may find this simplistic: evil is not always repaid. The Old Testament, too, knows well that the wicked often prosper and the righteous suffer. Yet violence breeds violence, and that is not the way to secure the peace for which the suffering multitudes long.

3 Easy forgiveness, cheap grace?

Judges 10:1–18

Among the major figures whose exploits are recounted at length are several 'minor judges', as they are often called, whose function seems to have been more strictly judicial and administrative. (For Samuel as a circuit judge, see 1 Samuel 7:15–17.) We meet two of them here—Tola and Jair. They seem to have been of local influence and we know little about them. Their details are recorded briefly in formulaic fashion (see also 12:8–15).

Israel's situation is tragic: the people are involved not in syncretism this time but in fullscale apostasy. They have abandoned the Lord for the supposed security of other gods. The days are dark, with the threat of Philistines in the south-west and Ammonites in the east, not only across the Jordan but right in their heartland (v. 9).

Israel knows what is wrong. Their other deities have proved ineffective so they turn back to Yahweh, God of last resort, looking for easy forgiveness and cheap grace. But choices always have consequences: 'Cry to the gods whom you have chosen,' comes the answer (v. 14). They have not learnt from past mercies; now they are to learn from present futility. Their prayer becomes desperate: 'Deliver us this day' (v. 15). Is this heartfelt repentance or 'the smug confidence of a spoiled child' (Polzin)? At any rate, they take action, discard the emblems of their faithlessness and commit themselves to the Lord.

So much for Israel's response, but what of Yahweh's? The Hebrew in verse 16 is unfortunately ambiguous (literally 'his soul was short at Israel's trouble'). Is he a compassionate God, no longer able to bear the sight of Israel's suffering (NRSV, NIV), or does it signify exasperation—'he had reached the limit of his patience', indignant at their calculated, self-serving repentance (Guest)? There is room here for reflection. For us, too, there is no cheap grace, only costly forgiveness won by Christ on the cross.

Is it significant that there is no further reference to prayer in this chapter? Instead the Israelites set out to find for themselves a deliverer for Gilead, the area in immediate danger. In the next chapter, they find a leader, Jephthah, whose story ends in tragedy.

4 Jephthah

Judges 11:1–28

Jephthah, like Abimelech, is an outsider, the son of a prostitute, rejected by his half-brothers and living on the fringes of society to the north of Gilead with outlaws as companions (v. 3: the Hebrew is derogatory—literally 'empty, worthless' folk). Among the judges, Jephthah is distinctive in his love of negotiation, first with the leaders of Gilead, then with the Ammonite enemy threatening invasion and finally (rashly) with Yahweh. Jephthah is never lost for words and motivating him throughout is his self-serving ambition.

'Come and be our commander' was the invitation from the elders of Gilead (v. 6), a military role to counter the immediate threat. Jephthah bargains for a better offer—to become 'head' over all the people (v. 8). Thus he achieves both military (*qatsin*) and civic status (*rosh*) and is careful to invoke the Lord's presence (v. 11).

Twice Jephthah sends envoys to the Ammonite king. Theirs is an ancient grudge reaching back to Moses' time: 'Israel… took away my land,' says the king (v. 13). Jephthah is understandably sarcastic: 'You've had 300 years to settle the score. Why now?' (v. 26). He is not only sarcastic but scathing too in what follows, for he speaks only of Moabites and Amorites, ignoring, in his long historical and geographical resumé, the very Ammonites whose king he is addressing. And here is a puzzle. When he refers to 'your god Chemosh' (v. 24), is Jephthah being ignorant or deliberately insulting to the Ammonites, treating them as simply part of Moab, whose deity was Chemosh? Milcom was the Ammonite god (1 Kings 11:5). They were a neighbouring people to Moab in the region of the Arnon. Whether or not his knowledge of history let him down,

certainly his defective theology—his ignorance of Yahweh and his ways—
did just that, first by treating Yahweh and Chemosh as two equal deities
('you possess what Chemosh gave you and we will possess what Yahweh
gave us': see v. 24), later by binding himself and his future irrevocably
with a foolish vow by which he thinks to manipulate Yahweh.

5 Destroyed by a senseless vow

Judges 11:29–40

The action takes place beyond the Jordan. It starts with an inrush of
power upon Jephthah. The expression 'spirit/wind (*ruah*) of the Lord'
denotes here a sensation of strength beyond the ordinary, without
implying any moral content. In the Old Testament, reference to the spirit
of the Lord occurs in a variety of contexts and it is the context that helps
to determine the meaning. Thus, in Hosea 13:15, the 'wind/spirit' of the
Lord is unambiguously destructive, like the dry east wind from the
desert. In contrast, the anointing by the spirit of the Lord in Isaiah
61:1–3 clearly has a moral content. Only twice in the Old Testament
does the expression 'holy spirit' occur (Isaiah 63:10–11).

Despite the sensation of power equipping him for the task in hand,
Jephthah strikes another bargain to secure his success, this time with the
Lord—a senseless, self-serving vow made at someone else's expense. Yet
Jephthah's rash words prove to be his own downfall: opening his mouth
to the Lord (as his daughter puts it, v. 36), he has closed down his
future—no child, no heir. Rash and foolish, his attempt to coerce the
Lord achieves his own destruction.

What did Jephthah expect when he made his dramatic vow?
Certainly not the fate of his only daughter. The Hebrew in verse 31 can
be translated 'whoever' (NRSV) or 'whatever' (NIV). Had he a slave in
mind—or an animal, perhaps? But the music and dancing of women
were customary in celebrating victory (1 Samuel 18:6), as Jephthah
must have known. The contrast between father and daughter, unnamed
as she is, is heartbreaking: she is courageous and self-giving, her father
concerned only for himself. Tearing his clothes in despair, he blames not
himself but his daughter for his own lost future. Verse 35 is totally self-
centred: 'You have brought *me* very low; you have become the cause of

great trouble to *me*.' The girl asks for time to lament, not for her undeserved death but for her unfulfilled life (Trible).

The narrator draws a veil over the whole shameful act, although the stark words, he 'did with her according to the vow' (v. 39) strike a chill. Human sacrifice was not acceptable to Yahweh (as is illustrated in the binding and deliverance of Isaac in Genesis 22). To our discomfort, Jephthah gains a place among the heroes of faith in Hebrews 11:32. His daughter remains nameless but not forgotten: 'she became a tradition in Israel' (v. 39, so Trible translates), her memory kept alive by other women.

6 Further bloodletting

Judges 12:1–15

The end of Jephthah's story is brief and brutal. Unlike his father Gideon when the Ephraimites confronted him with a similar complaint (8:1–3), Jephthah is undiplomatic. The verbal encounter that follows has a distinctly hostile tone. The threat of arson was not uncommon in the Judges' period, it seems (see 14:15). To judge from some news reports, is it much different today? Jephthah's response was merciless. Unity between the tribes was fast disintegrating, reaching its sordid climax in chapters 19—21.

The narrative is fascinating as a rare glimpse into variations of dialect among the Israelites. The Old Testament covers a vast period of time and a range of disparate tribes, separated by rugged mountainous terrain. That different dialects should have existed was inevitable, but for the most part they are now difficult for us to detect within the biblical text. In the face of the simple challenge offered to them (v. 6), the Ephraimites had no possible disguise. (Compare the similar challenge to Peter at Jesus' trial: 'your accent betrays you', Matthew 26:73.) No mercy was shown.

The brief notices of three 'minor judges' that follow Jephthah's violent story serve both to relieve the tension briefly and also, more significantly, to heighten the unbearable poignancy of its outcome. Jephthah loses his one and only daughter; Ibzan has 30 sons and 30 daughters, plus sons- and daughters-in-law (v. 9). The unusual inclusion of daughters and daughters-in-law in this verse is surely no accident. Likewise, Abdon's 40 sons and 30 grandsons are, for him, powerful guarantors of the future.

Note, too, that Jephthah was preceded by Jair, like him a Gileadite, but unlike him with 30 prosperous sons, hugely wealthy, possessing 30 donkeys and 30 towns or villages (10:4).

These brief notices, a formal record of a period in office and place of burial, bear similarities to the later king notices (for example, 1 Kings 14:19). These judges, like the kings, seem to follow each other in continuity. Judgeship was always 'teetering on the brink of kingship' (Guest) and eventually gave place to it.

Guidelines

This week's readings have allowed us a glimpse into an ancient society, vastly different in its mores from ours but alike in its insecurity, threatened by danger externally and by instability within. Society may have changed radically but, sadly, human nature has not. These gripping tales are rich in challenge and warning. Attitudes to women have changed rapidly in recent times, but even in the New Testament they are no longer nameless shadowy figures. Yet it is worth reflecting whether, to men and women alike, we always generously give credit where credit is due.

What of selfish, destructive ambition like Abimelech's, of courage to speak out as Jotham did in fear of his life, of treating the Lord as a God of last resort and offering superficial repentance as a way to easy forgiveness?

'Search *me*, O God, and know my heart; test *me* and know my thoughts… and lead *me* in the way everlasting' (Psalm 139:23–24).

30 JUNE–6 JULY

1 Samson

Judges 13:1–14

From birth to death, Samson's is an amazing story. To judge from its length, the ancient editor of Judges must have felt the same: in the arrangement of our Bibles it covers four whole chapters. Its continued influence in art and literature attests to the dramatic quality of the interplay between brute force and emotional weakness that marked Samson's life.

From the start—a woman visited by a divine messenger with the promise of a son—we know that this is to be no ordinary birth. Unlike Sarah (Genesis 18:10) and Hannah (1 Samuel 1:17), who also gave birth by divine promise, Samson's mother remains nameless throughout, identified only as Manoah's wife and relegated to the background in the patriarchal society of the time. Nevertheless, it is she, not Manoah, who is visited by the Lord's messenger. No casual visitation this, as she knows from the start, but a disturbing presence (v. 6: Hebrew literally 'very terrible'). Manoah seeks firsthand confirmation of his wife's tale (v. 8) and his prayer is heard, but it is to the woman that the angel comes again.

The Bible is emphatic in both Old and New Testaments that God communicates with humankind but in the Old Testament angelic messengers are often indistinguishable at first from humans. Here, however, the reader is let into the secret immediately—this is a divine visitation—and the woman senses an awesome presence 'like that of an angel of God' (v. 6). Manoah, whose name ironically means 'rest', seems a restless, uncertain figure, constantly seeking reassurance from his wife or from the messenger, but instructions to the woman are enough. No more is needed.

The strict rules surrounding the unborn infant alert us to the fact that this is to be an extraordinary child. The Nazirite vow (for details see Numbers 6:1–8) was normally a voluntary undertaking by an adult man or woman for a limited period. For Samson, it meant lifelong dedication even from the time of conception.

2 Common sense saves the day

Judges 13:15–25

Manoah has had only a secondary part to play thus far. Now he is eager for more of the action, reluctant to let this dramatic moment pass. Still unaware of the stranger's identity, he offers the customary hospitality and so the conversation with the angel is prolonged. Is Manoah still doubtful about the truth of it all? At first sight, verse 17 seems couched in positive terms: Manoah is eager to honour the messenger 'when your words come true'. Do we detect a more negative undertone here, though? What if his wife has been gullible? What if, eager for a child, she has been deceived? Who is this messenger? Who will be held accountable?

Then comes a hint of the messenger's identity, although Manoah does not yet perceive it. The name is too wonderful, too incomprehensible for human understanding. The word 'wonderful' used here (*pil'I*) is an unusual form of a commoner word and occurs elsewhere only in Psalm 139:6, referring there to Yahweh's inscrutability. Manoah doesn't like mystery. He wants to take control of the situation. The identity of the messenger matters to him.

At last the truth dawns—for Manoah, only with the angel's final disappearance. Manoah is terror struck: 'We shall sure die, for we have seen God' (v. 22). Once more, the woman takes the lead. There is a touch of humour here, as her common sense saves the day. She sees two cogent reasons for having no need to be afraid: the messenger's acceptance of their offering and the instructions about their future child. It was traditional in Israel for the mother to name her child. The final verse prepares us for the exploits to follow. The spirit (*ruah*) of the Lord began to 'stir' Samson (v. 25: a strong word in Hebrew, meaning 'impel, thrust'), violent like the wind (*ruah*).

3 Samson the trickster

Judges 14:1–20

The Samson stories have great entertainment value but they are more than that. They reflect the complexity of human personality—the dangerous combination of physical strength and emotional weakness in a hero singled out for consecration to the Lord and undone by self-gratification and his weakness for women. Only at the end of his story is he described as a judge, in the sense of being a deliverer of his people (15:20; 16:31). Many of his exploits are not on Israel's account but are the outcome of his own uncontrolled passions, although even here the narrator, in what seems to us a startling anthropomorphism (v. 4), affirms that Yahweh is ultimately in control.

Our expectations from the story of Samson' birth are disappointed and our hopes dashed. The Philistines are making dangerous inroads into Israel while Samson entangles himself with a Philistine woman. His parents are dismayed but Samson is self-willed. The comment 'Samson *went down* to Timnah' (v. 5) is more than a geographical statement. It has ominous overtones of spiritual decline (compare Jonah's descent in Jonah 1). This unconventional marriage outside the tribe was, in other respects, conventional, negotiated by the parents and publicly celebrated, unlike Samson's later more casual relationships. We have seen already the significant role of women in the narrative (namely the quickwitted woman with the millstone in 9:53 and Manoah's wife in ch. 13) who, although nameless and relegated to the background, yet displayed courage and presence of mind and, in some instances, changed the course of events. Here, in contrast, the woman desired by Samson is treated much like a chattel. No thought is given to her feelings, nor is she allowed a voice, although it must be noted that in the end she is not a passive victim but a deceiver (v. 17). 'Get her for me,' says Samson, 'because she pleases me' (v. 3) or, more literally, with a touch of irony, 'she's the right one for me' (NIV) (or even 'upright', Hebrew: *yesharah*).

Samson the trickster cannot resist a riddle (v. 14). The Philistines say to the woman, 'Coax (*patti*) your husband.' She 'nags' him (v. 17), a much more violent word—and Samson's riddle issues in escalating problems and finally in horrific violence.

4 A vicious circle

Judges 15:1–20

Samson is a law to himself, entirely at the whim of his sudden, uncontrolled emotions, impetuous and ruthless. Having deserted his bride in a fit of pique before even the traditional festivities were over, he decides to return to her. Here again, shocking our sensibilities, the wife and her sister are treated as objects to be traded for a man's satisfaction. From start to finish, however bizarre and exaggerated the details, this is a catalogue of tit-for-tat violence, all set in train by Samson's jealous rage. The Philistines, unable to wreak revenge on the powerful destroyer of their crops at the very moment of harvest (v. 1), attack the hapless woman and her father, causing more fiery deaths (v. 6). We shudder at the callous brutality of it all, sadly not unknown in today's world or in our own society. There are, however, more sensitive strands in the Old Testament (see Deuteronomy 22:1–4 concerning animals; 16:11–14 with regard to women, and especially the book of Ruth).

The repeated references to the Philistines throughout the story never let us forget the identity of Israel's dangerous enemy at the time, yet it is with a Philistine woman that Samson has entangled himself and he will do so again with Delilah. He never learns.

A memorable little rhyme playing on two Hebrew words (*hamor*) identical in sound, meaning both 'heap' and 'donkey', accounts for the name of Ramoth-lehi, 'hill of the jawbone', a place of uncertain location:

With the jawbone (lehi) *of a donkey, heaps upon heaps,*
with the jawbone of a donkey I have slain a thousand men (v. 16).

Even Samson, for all his strength, needs resources beyond his own. Thirst defeats him and at last he cries out to God.

Was there more to Samson's story than we have seen so far, bringing deliverance, not disaster? The end of our chapter hints perhaps at this— 'he judged Israel in the days of the Philistines twenty years'—but this concluding summary is not the end. There is the dramatic Delilah episode to follow.

5 Delilah, a dangerous infatuation

Judges 16:1–17

Judges 15:20 looked like a neat ending to Samson's story, but there is more drama, more tragedy and triumph to come. This is ancient oral tradition committed to writing probably around the tenth century BC, and sometimes the seams show. In fact, there is something of a pattern common to chapters 15 and 16. Besides their almost identical endings, 'he judged Israel twenty years', they each conclude with a rare admission of Samson's weakness and ultimate reliance on Yahweh for help (16:17), but there the parallels end. Both prayers are answered: in the first, 'his spirit (NIV: 'strength') returned, and he revived' (15:19); in the second, triumph spells his death.

Samson refused to learn from experience. Three times he was involved with Philistine women when his vocation was to deliver Israel from 40 years of Philistine oppression. For him, there was sadly no match between public duty and private life. Time after time he knowingly put himself in a corner, confident that his superior strength would secure his escape. His relationship with Delilah is described as 'love' (v. 4) and here the infatuation proved irresistible. This independent woman, identified not by any relationship to a man as daughter, wife or mother but solely by her own name, lays her plans for financial gain. Samson's sheer recklessness is breathtaking. With overweening hubris, he believes that his physical prowess is at his own disposal, not as a gift to be used for the sake of his oppressed people. But God is not 'a god of the gaps', a God of last resort when more than human help is needed. He is the Lord of life, of our whole life's commitment.

Where was the Lord in Samson's thinking? Dedicated before birth, even before conception, this meant little to Samson. Delilah's nagging took precedence over his relationship with God. Samson was obtuse, playing fast and loose with his commitment. A woman had coaxed an earlier riddle from him and betrayed him (14:16–17); Delilah repeats the process with far more serious consequences.

6 A fateful choice

Judges 16:18–31

Samson's was a noble calling, to deliver God's people from years of oppression—in short, to be their saviour. His extraordinary strength was a gift suited to his task, not his by right. What solemn, doomladen words are these: 'he did not know that the Lord had left him' (v. 20). Delilah and the Philistine chiefs are all around him but Samson is alone. Committing himself to a woman who has deceived him, he has neglected the Lord who had sustained him. Choice always brings consequences.

For the writer, the conflict was not merely Israel versus the Philistines but Yahweh versus Dagon. (To illustrate this theme, see the graphic account in 1 Samuel 5:1–4.) There is powerful irony here. In the very act of their praising Dagon for victory (a ditty whose rhythm is obscured in the NRSV, vv. 23–24), Yahweh has the last word. The foolish hero dies at the moment of his triumph but, for now, the Philistine threat is over. Down the years, Samson's story has proved an inspiration, a reminder that it is never too late for the Lord to act.

Samson's false choices destroyed his life. There was triumph at the end but, for him, extreme humiliation. Abimelech was ashamed to have died at a woman's hand (9:54). The heroic Samson was reduced to grinding corn (16:21), a humble domestic task, the work of women or animals. The description of Samson as a judge/deliverer at the end of his story accords oddly with the content of his exploits, which seem more often to have been carried out for his own renown than for his people's rescue. Perhaps this is a reminder that there was more to his story than the few dramatic displays narrated here. Certainly the writer of Hebrews counted him among the heroes of faith (Hebrews 11:32).

Guidelines

The Samson narrative is powerful storytelling—folktales embellished over the years with telling and retelling, stories of heroism and brutality, gripping and horrifying in turn—but it is more than that. For the ancient editor who included it in the story of Israel's life with God, it had a theological message, a warning of the perennial temptation to let commitment to God slip into the background and the exigencies of a situation take precedence.

What are 21st-century Christian readers to make of it? We can revel in the storyteller's art and look with detached interest at ancient attitudes to God or we can face their uncomfortable challenge, despite the gulf of centuries, to our own relationships and our balancing of human desires with divine calling. Whatever our response to the Samson stories, the fact that he was more victorious when helpless in death than he was in life points us to our greater Deliverer and his dying cry of victory, 'It is finished' (John 19:30). Samson's ultimate victory was won, however, amid massive destruction of human life: Christ's victory offers life and freedom for all.

FURTHER READING

P. Deryn Guest, 'Judges' in *Eerdmans Commentary on the Bible* (eds. James D.G. Dunn and John W. Rogerson), Eerdmans, 2003.

A.D.H. Mayes, *Judges* (Old Testament Guides), Sheffield Academic Press, 1989.

Phyllis Trible, *Texts of Terror: Literary–Feminist Readings of Biblical Narratives*, Augsberg Fortress, 1984, on the story of Jephthah's daughter.

THE PASTORAL EPISTLES

Most people think 1 Timothy, 2 Timothy and Titus are the same kind of animal—almost different chapters of the same book. It's certainly true that they are all letters. They seem to be from the same person, and two of them are addressed to one individual. They have some common themes, particularly the practice of ministry (hence the title 'pastoral'). They seem to come from somewhere near the end of the New Testament period when churches are becoming more established. There seems to be some development of thought from the earlier and main Pauline epistles to this final collection.

The differences and similarities between these letters and the earlier letters from Paul have led to debate about whether they are from a later period or by a different author writing in Paul's name. In the end, this is an insoluble question. In these notes I will assume that the letters are what they claim to be: messages from Paul, probably at a late stage in his ministry, to two of his associates, Timothy and Titus.

In one sense these letters form a neat group, but in another they are quite different from each other. I like to think of 1 Timothy as a big, public letter. It is addressed to Timothy in his public role. It is the kind of letter that is meant to be read aloud in congregations and form a guide to pastoral practice and doctrine across a group of churches. It contains concise, well-distilled practical wisdom for sustaining church life.

2 Timothy is very different: it is addressed to Timothy as an individual at a particular moment of crisis in his life and ministry. These are not words to a young minister but to someone in midlife, addressing issues of failure and re-engagement. The letter to Titus changes gear again. It's a 'bits and pieces' kind of letter: a scattergun of sayings and advice, less grand in scale and considered than 1 Timothy, less personal than 2 Timothy, but with real pearls of wisdom at its heart.

If there is a wider common theme to the letters and these notes, it is not so much about starting new things but about sustaining them, whether in our communities or in our personal lives. The pastorals are about how to develop churches and people who persevere and who can live against the grain of their culture. Interested? Then read on.

1 How long should I stay?

1 Timothy 1

Should I go or should I stay? A key question for any Christian minister, lay or ordained, is how long to remain involved in a community or piece of ministry. If you leave or withdraw too early, then everything may fall apart. If you stay too long, you may create cultures of dependence and not give space for new leaders to emerge.

Timothy has been left behind in Ephesus to watch over and consolidate the development of the church there. If you don't know the story of its founding, take a few moments to read through Acts 19. The Ephesian church was founded in a cosmopolitan city—a meeting point of Jewish and Greek cultures. It appears that Timothy has had enough of Ephesus and now wants to move on. The opening verse of the letter, after the greeting, makes clear (for the second time) that he needs to stay where he is for a while longer. The young churches are not yet mature enough to be left to their own devices. The letter will unpack what needs to happen and what people and disciplines need to be put in place.

We will hear much that is positive in the letter but first Paul spells out the negative. Unless Timothy agrees to stay, false teaching is likely to gain a hold. There was, no doubt, a lot of false teaching about Ephesus, which contained a maelstrom of conflicting views from those on the fringes of Judaism to those steeped in occult practices. Paul fights to keep the church centred on the heart of the gospel of Jesus. The aim of Christian learning and teaching is not knowledge for its own sake but love (v. 5). When we get to heaven, according to Thomas à Kempis, we will not be asked how much we have read but how we have loved others. It takes time and sound teaching to see this message take root in the lives of new believers.

Paul's wisdom cuts to the heart of the false teaching because it is centred on his own experience of God's grace and forgiveness and the first 'trustworthy saying' of these letters: 'Christ Jesus came into the world to save sinners' (v. 15). Nothing else is needed. The call to follow Christ is the call to remember that central truth each day, and to respond to God's grace in love and praise.

2 First things first

The gospel is the centre of the Christian life, but what are the things that bring stability and good order to a Christian community—the habits that Timothy is charged with developing before he can move on? The first priority is bringing order to the worship of the community. It is especially important that the worship is characterized by prayers and that these prayers are set within a view of the world that sees God as Lord of the whole creation, a God who wants everyone to be saved.

To those of us who have lived our lives in stable Christian communities with good habits of worship, this may seem a most basic instruction—not worth repeating or emphasizing. Yet these principles become vital again in thinking about developing new communities— fresh expressions of church. They are also extremely important in watching over the worship of existing congregations. I sat with a vicar at supper this evening who admitted that the element of intercession has been all but squeezed out of the worship in his church by blocks of choruses and personal ministry time. Paul would have something to say about that.

So far, so good. What of the second half of the chapter, which gives different instructions to men and women? Can that be right in the 21st century? Opinions differ on the interpretation of these verses, but it is clear to most commentators that here the author is changing an existing early practice—well attested in the New Testament—of women sharing in teaching and recognized ministries. One recent commentator, Howard Marshall, argues persuasively that he must be doing so for local reasons. A particular scandal and wrong practice has arisen in Ephesus, perhaps linked with the cult of Artemis in the city. The women are dominating the life of the church (the word translated 'to have authority' can carry this much stronger meaning). There is a hint also of sexual licence in the instructions to both men and women about their manner of prayer and their dress codes. The verses therefore speak to this specific situation and correct an imbalance for that time and for that place. They need to be applied and understood today against the background of the whole of the New Testament and the liberation offered to women as well to men.

3 The household of God

First, Timothy has to see to the ordering of worship. His next task is to set ministry on firm foundations. He needs to appoint a new bishop, perhaps to take his own place in overseeing the whole community. He also needs to appoint some new deacons, men and women who will be ambassadors for the church and agents of God's love in the wider community. These workers are in addition to the presbyters or elders whom we read about in chapter 5, who labour in preaching and teaching. Perhaps Timothy has written to Paul asking for advice on these appointments.

The Christian community discovered at an early stage that it was helpful to the whole Church to set aside people for particular ministries —although the exact pattern of these ministries would evolve and change over time. Such people are normally set aside through prayer and the laying on of hands, but first they go through a process of selection and testing by the whole community. The pattern established by the apostles prevails today.

Note that Paul does not provide a job description for the post of bishop or deacon (fascinating though that would be). Instead he sets out the qualities needed in the character of the people appointed. Christian ministry is always about who we are before it is about what we do. These lists remain helpful in determining who should be entrusted with responsibility among God's people.

Notice that one image of God's Church runs through the chapter: together we are God's 'household'. (The picture is of the large extended household of the ancient world, not the nuclear family of today.) The head of the household is not any Christian minister but God himself, while different ministers take on responsibilities according to their own qualities and gifts. Together the whole household bears witness to the centrality and truth of the gospel (vv. 16–17).

How do our own households and the churches of which we are part bear witness to this truth?

4 Example first, teaching second

Timothy's imaginary letter to Paul runs on. 'What should I look for in a new bishop and new deacons? Some teachers have arrived, saying we are not strict enough in our faith. I feel so inadequate, Paul. Come quickly.'

Paul patiently continues his advice. 'There's lots of false teaching around: take no notice. Marriage and food are created by God. As for you, Timothy, be encouraged!'

Most of this chapter is direct advice to Timothy as a minister, feeling inadequate for the challenges before him. Through Timothy, Paul is also offering his wisdom to those who are drawn into the ministries of bishop and deacon that he has just described. Growth in godliness is like physical training, says Paul. It will be hard work and demanding but hugely valuable.

If we want to serve God in any situation, we must first be concerned with the kind of example we are giving to others. We live the Christian faith before we can teach it. Our example will include the way we talk, the things we do and the virtues we practise (love, faith and purity in this list: v. 12).

Good teaching can be effective only when built on the foundation of a transparent and good life. Most patterns of Christian ministry, from Jesus onwards, have had ministers living among and being part of the congregation to whom they preach, rather than visiting from time to time. Integrity is the foundation.

Once he has paid attention to his own life, Timothy must also focus on the public reading of scripture and teaching. It seems that he is shrinking from this responsibility, perhaps intimidated by the false teachers who are pushing in ahead of him and misleading the congregation. Not for the last time, Paul encourages Timothy to overcome his fears and reapply himself to his calling.

How do our fear and sense of inadequacy get in the way of serving God and the exercise of the gifts we have been given? How can we overcome that fear this day?

5 Tough love

A minister in a growing church faces many problems. 'How do I relate to different groups within the life of the church? How do we manage the relief we give to the poor? What about paying staff members? All of this is really stressing me out, Paul.'

Paul returns to the picture of the Church as God's household, encouraging Timothy to think of how he relates to the different members of his family and to speak to members of the church in the same ways— to an older man as his father and so on. This is good advice for every member of any church, not just a minister. Respect and purity should characterize all our relationships in God's household.

The long passage about widows is a wonderful example of tough love, which is not in the least bit sentimental when it comes to assessing practical need. Paul is all too familiar with people's tendency to exploit the generosity of others. The Church as the household of God needs to support those who have no other income or means of sustaining themselves, but care needs to be taken that people do not exploit this generosity—otherwise the whole system will collapse.

It is expected that people will support their own families and that the charity of the church community will be a last resort. That charity is also offered, in this instance, only to those who are members of God's household and whose lives are aligned with the expectations of that membership.

God's household also needs to take care how it treats those who serve the community, especially in preaching and teaching. Normally, these servants are to be supported financially in their work, protected against slander, investigated impartially when they are accused (as happens in every kind of church) and, because of the responsibility they carry, publicly rebuked when they do wrong. Again there is a tenderness and care for those who offer ministry, combined with a very practical realism: even people who hold responsibility are fallible and make many mistakes.

Oversight of all this is a demanding and difficult task. Those who undertake it on our behalf need our support and encouragement. They also need to be gentle with themselves as people loved by God. What can we do today to support and encourage those who lead our own community?

6 Godliness with contentment

1 Timothy 6

This chapter deals first with one particular, demanding set of relationships within the household—those who were members of the Church but were enslaved by Christian masters. In that generation, slavery itself was not challenged but the relationships between slave and master were to be transformed. In later generations, of course, slavery itself was seen to be contrary to Christ's law. We can profitably apply the insights of these verses to Christians who are members of the same church and find themselves also working together for the same company. We remain believers and part of God's household in every part of our lives.

In those communities, what do we need to be happy? Churches, like any other community, can easily be poisoned by greed. Our consumer age perhaps needs to hear these words more than any other in these epistles: 'for we brought nothing into the world, so that we can take nothing out of it; but if we have food and clothing, we will be content with these' (vv. 7–8). This was the way of Jesus who, as far as we know, owned nothing.

We should do what we can, then, to purge ourselves of the love of money (v. 10), for it will lead to all kinds of wrongdoing. If we happen to be rich ourselves and have more than we need for the basic necessities of life, we should see this condition as an occasion for thanksgiving to God and the opportunity to do good in the world.

Timothy is to put the desire for wealth out of his mind for the sake of his ministry. Instead he is to pursue other qualities, which are more vital for his life now and the life to come: righteousness, godliness, faith, love, endurance and gentleness (v. 11). He is encouraged to see his life not as a place of stillness and peace but as a battle to be fought, following the example of his Lord until that Lord returns.

Guidelines

What are the things you need to be happy? To live in contemporary Britain is to be continually exposed to the messages of advertising and a consumer culture. The rhythm of that culture is in one way the very opposite of the rhythm of the New Testament. Our culture works by continually stimulating the appetite for more possessions. Our very economy would grind to a halt without the urge to acquire more things and more money.

Some years ago, I had the immense privilege of teaching and reading the book of Acts with a small group of students from all over the world. We had someone in the class from China, someone from Africa and someone who had served as a missionary in South America, as well as people from different parts of Europe and North America. Reading the story of the early Church with them, I realized that I had missed the significant emphasis in Luke's story on the sharing of wealth and possessions. There is a real and practical generosity throughout the book.

However, the foundation of that generosity cannot be the desire to acquire more and more. The foundation has to be the picture of sufficiency and contentment found in 1 Timothy 6: if we have food and clothing (and, we presume, shelter), that is enough for us to be content. This seems to me to be a key lesson for today's Christians to learn and to teach in our discipleship. Have we learnt it? Are we teaching it to others as Timothy taught both by word and example?

1 My beloved child

2 Timothy 1

We now begin a different letter addressed to a different situation. 2 Timothy is one of the tenderest and most personal documents in the New Testament. The questions Timothy faces in the first epistle are about whether or not to move on and about how to consolidate the work that has begun in the church in Ephesus. Now the emphasis is entirely on his own ministry, from the beginning to end of the letter.

I have read the letter many times over the last 30 years and I have gradually come to the conclusion that it must be read against a background of real distress and, probably, persecution against the Christians in Ephesus. Timothy seems to have failed in some way to stand firm in his confession of faith. As leader of the church there, and one of Paul's associates, he would be in the front line in any time of difficulty. I suspect that he has not stood firm and has withdrawn from suffering.

In this second letter, Paul attempts to reach out to his associate, to bring him words of love and comfort and to strengthen him in the new trials that will come. Timothy is now called 'my beloved child' (v. 2). Paul assures Timothy of his constant prayers, day and night, as he recalls Timothy's tears (v. 4). He reminds Timothy of the faith of his own family and the depth of his discipleship and invites him gently to rekindle the gift that he has been given. Cowardice (even in the face of persecution) has no place among the gifts of the Spirit. We are not talking here about the natural apprehension we feel when faced with a difficult task but about our response to danger for the sake of our faith.

All parents, whether physical or spiritual, want to spare their beloved children from suffering or harm. How costly it must have been, then, for Paul to urge Timothy not to be ashamed of 'the testimony about our Lord'—a testimony that could have cost him his life—but to 'join with me in suffering for the gospel' (v. 8). Paul appeals to his own example as a prisoner in Rome: in this, also, Timothy is to imitate his mentor and be unafraid of arrest. Paul appeals also to Christ, who has abolished death and promises resurrection. He is able to commit Timothy's safety and the progress of the gospel to this risen Christ.

If we are right to imagine the letter as written against this background, its theme is the cost of Christian commitment—taking our share of suffering as servants of Christ.

2 Be strong in the Lord

2 Timothy 2

Paul continues to instruct his beloved child and prepare him for the testing to come. Timothy must pass on what he has heard to others (v. 2). This is not simply a general instruction for ministry but a specific one in case he is imprisoned or killed. All Christian ministry involves some kind of cost, and the cost for the soldier is the risk of death.

Where does the strength come from to re-enter the fray and take a share in suffering again? For Paul, it comes from remembering Jesus and the promise of resurrection: 'If we have died with him, we will also live with him' (v. 11). For us, it comes also from the example of Paul and others who have gone this way before us.

The three metaphors for Christian service all turn around the expectation that suffering will be part of the Christian and ministerial life. The soldier's suffering (vv. 3–4) is to endure personal risk and even death as part of fulfilling his role. This is the situation that Timothy faces now. The athlete's hardship (v. 5) lies in the demands of training and preparation in order to be able to compete at the highest level. The Christian must live to the highest standards at all times. The farmer's suffering (v. 6) is in the sheer labour required to see a crop grow. At different times in our lives and ministries, we may face each of these kinds of endurance.

There are many ways to share in suffering for Christ. It is all too easy, in midlife or mid-ministry, to step away from the costliness of living as a Christian and making sacrifices for the gospel. Perhaps we justify it to ourselves in a range of different ways. If we are in that place, then the message of this letter to us is to step back up to the plate—to take up the cross again—to take our share in suffering like a soldier risking his life in battle, an athlete maintaining the discipline of training or a farmer investing in the harvest to come.

A life that is centred on living for God is focused: there is no time or space for profane chatter or trivial argument about secondary matters of faith. There is a call to be dedicated to God's service in everything we are able to do.

3 Look at me

2 Timothy 3

In order to live well, we need to be absolutely realistic about the world. The wise Christian man or woman will not be naive about evil. In the days between the resurrection of Jesus and his return (the last days), there will be much wickedness and deceit, and the Church itself is not immune. Even Christian ministers will go astray (vv. 1–9).

In most of us, perhaps, there is a strong temptation to naivete and idealism when we think about the Church and Christian ministry. That naivete can lead to the depths of disappointment and despair when our illusions are shattered. Paul will have none of it. Those who share in ministry with him must be prepared for the depth of wickedness they will encounter.

How is the Christian to navigate through these troubled and confusing times? How are we to keep faith alive and live well? Where in particular are we to find strength and inspiration in those moments when we are almost overwhelmed by all we have to do or the suffering in the world?

Paul writes to Timothy in just such a moment. He is not afraid to point to his own example as an older Christian and a more experienced minister: 'you have observed my teaching, my conduct, my aim in life... my steadfastness, my persecutions, and my suffering' (vv. 10–11). From Paul's perspective, a degree of suffering and persecution is not exceptional but normal in the Christian life. Yet Timothy must remember as well that on many occasions when Paul has faced imprisonment and death he has been delivered by the Lord and preserved for future ministry.

How can we navigate these troubled times? By looking to the example of those who have gone before us and by putting down deep roots in the faith and especially in the scriptures (vv. 16–17). It is through a lifelong engagement with the 'God-breathed' writings and the example of the saints of God that we are able to find which way to go. It is from these two sources that we gain the strength to keep going and remain faithful to Christ even in the most testing of moments.

4 The final charge

2 Timothy 4

In the final chapter, we discover that even as Paul writes these words of comfort and challenge to Timothy, he himself is on trial for his life. The letter is written in the knowledge that he may never write another. There is no certainty that he will see Timothy again in this life. He describes his situation in beautiful images and memorable words: 'I am already being poured out as a libation, and the time of my departure has come. I have fought the good fight, I have finished the race, I have kept the faith' (vv. 6–7). Here Paul echoes two of the three images in 2:4–5. He describes himself in verse 17 as having been rescued from the lion's mouth: a literal reference to Christians being fed to wild beasts in the arena. His trial is not going well (v. 16) and he has no one to stand by him.

This provides a different context for the encouragement to Timothy to endure suffering faithfully. Here is no armchair general, a long way from the front line. Here is someone who is indeed following his own advice.

Paul's solemn charge to Timothy in the opening verses of the chapter therefore carries a special weight: 'proclaim the message' (v. 2). He must fulfil this ministry, as Paul himself has done, whether the time is favourable or unfavourable. He must convince, rebuke and encourage with the utmost patience and persistence (vv. 2–3). This is Timothy's gift and calling, confirmed by many witnesses and through the laying on of hands. Whatever the cost and the risk, he must find the resources to return to this calling and find within it the fulfilment of his life and ministry.

Paul's command to Timothy at the beginning of the first letter is to stay where he is. Now he urges him to come swiftly to join him (v. 21)—most probably in Rome. Both the joys and the pain of human fellowship shine through the final verses. There are notes about those who have been faithful to Paul and those who have abandoned him, reminders about parchment and a cloak—the signs of an ordinary life at the end of an extraordinary letter.

May God grant to each of us the grace to fulfil our own ministry, whatever that may be, and to run the race he has set before us.

5 Mission impossible?

Titus 1:1—2:6

Titus is another close associate of Paul, apparently left behind in Crete (1:5) and entrusted with an extremely difficult and challenging task. He has to 'put in order what remained to be done' and take the new churches there on from the foundations laid by Paul. This letter, like 1 Timothy, is meant as a public document: Paul introduces himself formally and the instructions about church life and ministry are clearly intended to be read to the whole community. There is no hint here of the suffering and persecution that run through 2 Timothy.

Titus faces the 'ordinary' challenges of pastoral ministry rather than the extraordinary trials of persecution. Nevertheless, those challenges amount to a mission that, humanly, speaking seems impossible. As in

Jesus' parable of the wheat and tares, the church in Crete is full of people who are 'rebellious… idle talkers and deceivers' (v. 10). Paul is startlingly frank about the moral condition of the Cretans as a whole. The people whom Titus must teach to be Christians are, by their own admission, habitual liars, brutes and gluttons. The centre of Titus' ministry is not to be comfort or encouragement but rebuke and confrontation (v. 13).

What is the antidote to all of this and the way forward in a massive task? Titus must first appoint appropriate ministers to share his own responsibilities and consolidate the work. Again, as in 1 Timothy, he is to look for people of virtue to be elders and to be bishop (vv. 5–9). The bishop in particular must present a good example in the areas of moral weakness that Paul has identified in the culture of the island: he must not be addicted to wine (mentioned a number of times through the letter) and should be well equipped to preach and teach.

In chapter 2, Paul tells Titus and other ministers to give different instructions and examples to the different groups in the community. One of the most challenging aspects of Christian ministry is that all teaching must be carefully applied to a range of different people and situations. The older men have to learn new habits of restraint and prudence. The older women are to be reverent and not slaves to drink. They must become teachers of the faith, particularly to the younger women (contrast this with the very different situation of 1 Timothy 2). The younger men are simply urged to be self-controlled as the first step in their own growth and transformation.

Paul and Titus recognize that what they are about is not simply the conversion of individuals but also the transformation of a whole culture on the island, to bring new hope, stability and a better way of living. Is this our vision for the ministry of the Church in our own day in the cultures to which we carry the gospel? The tools will be the same.

6 Living against the flow

Titus 2:7—3:15

For centuries in Britain, to live as a Christian has been to live with the flow of our society. Sundays and holy days have been legally protected. Christian ethics and lifestyle have been aligned with the ethics of our culture. As our society changes, we are now beginning to get a glimpse of what it will mean once again to live against the flow as a Christian disciple.

This was the kind of living that Titus was to encourage by his own example and through his teaching (2:7–8). The Christian community was not strong enough to challenge the institution of slavery. The best that could be done was to encourage those who were slaves to bear witness to Christ within their own situation through obedience and faithfulness, rather than taking advantage of their masters.

The same principle is to apply to the whole community within society as a whole (3:1–2). The Christians are to do their utmost to live as an obedient and peaceable minority within the context of Cretan society, commending themselves by their good deeds and harmony with one another. Like Christians in every age, they are to centre their own lives on the great truths of the gospel—that Christ has given himself for us to redeem us from slavery and purify us as a holy people (2:14) and that our salvation is not because of anything we have done but because of his mercy, through waters of rebirth and renewal by the Holy Spirit (3:5). These core doctrines are at the heart of transformation and changed lives.

Living as a minority and bearing witness to Christ in a hostile culture demand a particular discipline of unity in the Christian community: it is vital not to quarrel about secondary matters ('stupid controversies, genealogies, dissensions, and quarrels about the law', 3:9). These quarrels do immense harm to the Christian witness that we offer to the love of Christ. They also weaken the already fragile Christian community. Like every Christian minister, from time to time Titus has to exercise discipline, particularly with those who are divisive. After two warnings he is to have nothing more to do with such a person (v. 10).

The letter concludes, like 2 Timothy, with a range of personal notes and then what seems like an afterthought but could be a whole curriculum for Christian discipleship: the need to continue to do good, to provide for daily necessities and not to live an unproductive life. It ends as it begins, with grace.

Guidelines

To live as a disciple is consciously to take up our cross and follow Jesus (Matthew 16:24). There is no way to read the New Testament and escape the conclusion that sharing in suffering, in some measure, is the lot of those who would follow Christ. There are many joys, many gains and many treasures that far outweigh the cost, but there is no disguising the fact that suffering is part of the package.

Paul, following the pattern of all the apostles, is very clear about this with his early converts. When he retraces his steps with Barnabas after the first missionary journey, we get a glimpse of the course content in his early discipleship material: 'We must go through many hardships to enter the kingdom of God' (Acts 14:22, NIV).

The pastoral epistles, particularly 2 Timothy, reinforce that picture, but I wonder how much this notion of cost and suffering forms part of our own expectations of the Christian life or our instruction of others today. In a world in which it seems hard to communicate the gospel, it is tempting to focus on the easy or attractive parts of Christianity. To parody, our teaching can easily seem to say, 'Come to Jesus, join our wonderful church and all your problems will be solved.' Such a rosy picture of faith and Christian life seems to satisfy for a time but sooner or later it is eroded or shattered by the actual experience of living and of an imperfect church.

If we are to learn the lessons of the pastoral epistles, we need to be clear with ourselves and with others that Jesus' invitation is to live a difficult and demanding life in an imperfect and continually fallible community of other believers. It is meant to be a life of wonderful purpose. It is meant to be the life intended for us by God. It is meant to be a life based on truth and lived in the hope of new life beyond death. It is also, however, a life and a calling that will stretch us and test us in a range of different ways.

In living such a life and being honest about all that it means, we should expect times when we, like Timothy, are tempted to put down the cross and step back from the cost—to settle for less than the best. In those moments, we, like Paul, need to extend to each other tender love and care, reminders of the past when we have walked faithfully with Christ and promises of God's hope in Christ. At those times, also, we may need to hear Christ's gentle call to take up the cross once more and play our part, whether in the intensity of a farmer's labours, the endurance of an athlete's training or the risk of a soldier going to battle.

EZEKIEL

Ezekiel is an extraordinary book. Set at the pivotal moment of Old Testament history, the exile (most agree, between the years 593 and 571 BC), it speaks into a time when traditional theology is being shaken to its very core with the loss of all that the people believed God had given to them: Jerusalem, king, land and temple. The book is addressed to the exiles in Babylon, who are struggling to understand where God is in the midst of such devastation. They have been estranged from the land, the temple and all familiar forms of worship; have they also been estranged from God? During this traumatic period, a number of great theologians arise—not systematic theologians, seeking to present a tidy theology written in libraries or studies, but prophetic theologians, speaking to a people in a tumultuous time of devastation, seeking to make sense of a situation of extreme chaos. One of these remarkable prophetic theologians is the priest Ezekiel, lover of the holy city and the temple, of whom we know nothing beyond the remarkable words of the book attributed to him.

Ezekiel's is a unique voice, whose strangeness and violence equal the strangeness and violence of the dreadful situation into which he is prophesying. Repetitive and detailed to the point of obsession, resonating with blood and aggression, overflowing with bizarre sign-actions, personifications and visions, there is no underestimating the challenge of this writing. It is at times deeply disturbing. Yet, at the same time, there is an incomparable magnificence to these words, which witness powerfully to God's unutterable beauty, and there is no doubt that this book contributed significantly to the birth of a new people of God from the wreckage of the exile. We are about to encounter one of the greatest theologians of the Old Testament.

Key to Ezekiel's theology is what Paul Joyce has called its 'radical theocentricity'. In this time of immense turbulence, the prophetic theologian responds by foregrounding God's power, will and authority to an extraordinary degree. Who is in control of this situation? God is! Who brought the exile about? God did! Who alone has the power to bring about restoration? God does! All is done for the 'sake of my name', to the point where we could say that the people of God are left in the shadows of the book, often with disquieting consequences. Throughout the first section, they are portrayed as having provoked God to fury through their abominations and betrayals. This is a book of extremes, where the possibility of balance or holding the middle ground is ruled out from the very outset. This radical prophet will go to extraordinary lengths, even rewriting the story of God's people, to convey the imperative message that in the midst of exile and destruction the God of Judah is present and in full control.

If the book of Ezekiel can appear wild, even frenzied, at times, it is among the most carefully structured books in the Old Testament. Its threefold structure meticulously and painstakingly leads us through (1) judgment on Judah and Jerusalem (chs. 1—24); (2) oracles against foreign nations (chs. 25—32); (3) restoration and hope (chs. 33—48). The fact that hope will finally blossom is worth remembering when we are in the midst of the darkest places of chapters 1—24, which witness powerfully to the prophet's profound ability to communicate the desolation, violence and trauma of what it means to be in exile.

1 God in exile

Ezekiel 1:1–28

After three verses of carefully dated introduction, Ezekiel's first vision erupts from our pages with astonishing power, streaming forth with an overwhelming intensity of evocative description. Most agree that there is no Old Testament 'theophany' (vision of God) to equal this. It is an extraordinary introduction to an extraordinary book.

God arrives in Babylon in his chariot of fire. Stunned and shaken, the prophet struggles for words, leaving translators and readers also reeling in the wake of the intensity of the experience. If the language seems strange in English, it is even more tangled in Hebrew, with spelling mistakes, confusions of gender and number, strange grammatical forms and clipped sentences, leading to countless scholarly emendations and alternatives. The prophet is struggling to bring words into conformity to describe the indescribable, and shattering them in the process. Note the sheer number of words such as 'like', 'appearance of', 'something like' and 'likeness of' strewn throughout the narrative. Scholars compare Isaiah 6:1's sparse 'I saw the Lord' with Ezekiel 1's climactic final verse: 'This was the appearance of the likeness of the glory of the Lord'. Even as he describes, the prophet is distancing his words from being an actual description of God, whom words cannot contain, and as he wrestles to make language speak the unspeakable, we could say that we are left as stunned as the prophet.

If this is an astonishing vision, it needed to be—addressed to a people stranded far (by traditional theology) from God's presence. The prophet's message is clear. The God of Judah has burst free from the limits supposed for him of temple, Jerusalem and land, to erupt forth in the midst of this land of captivity in unutterable glory. Ezekiel the priest will continue to long for Jerusalem, temple and land: this is a book that recognizes people's intuitive link with geography, familiarity and tradition. Nevertheless, the overwhelming recognition spills forth from the very opening pages: God is greater than all of these, transcending all boundaries that humans set. We are compelled to ask: where are Jerusalem and the temple for us—the places, routines, forms of worship, songs or prayers through which we normally encounter God? Are we, like Ezekiel, open to perceiving the presence of God beyond them, in the strangest of places and among the most unlikely of people, even where we have believed God cannot possibly be treading?

2 Swallowing the scroll

Ezekiel 2:8—3:3

Ezekiel's vision continues with his commission, which is equally dramatic. An unidentified voice (God or the spirit?) speaks, ordering Ezekiel to swallow whatever is given to him. Before the terrified prophet appears a scroll, written all over both front and back: no room remains for dissent, additions or interpretation. It is filled with 'lamentation and mourning and woe' (v. 2). The three-times repetition of the command dramatically captures the prophet's appalled hesitation at stomaching such a message on behalf of his people. We can only imagine his bewilderment and relief when, on consuming the scroll, it becomes as sweet as honey in his mouth.

The story of the horrified prophet swallowing the scroll appears at the beginning of this book for a reason. Ezekiel is being presented to us as a vital model for reading, for Ezekiel is itself a scroll overflowing with 'lamentation, mourning and woe', among the most troubling works in the Old Testament. Like the prophet, we are carefully counselled not to look at its surface level only, for then we might either hesitate to accept its dreadful words, baulking at their harshness, or attempt straight-forwardly to translate their complex message into our lives in in-appropriate ways. Instead, we are challenged to take courage and—even while aware of this scroll's dreadful exterior—to receive its words deep within ourselves, not fast-forwarding through key passages when they become discomforting but staying with them in their pain. It is only then that we might experience the sweetness of their taste.

The model that the prophet offers is not only relevant for reading Ezekiel but also provides us with a more general challenge about how we respond to God in our daily lives. Do we only orientate ourselves towards portrayals of God that will give us 'cheap hope' and comfort, without the unsettling challenge that we might need to hear? Do we keep what God might be saying to us at arm's length, assuming that we know what it is about and not allowing it to go deep within us, where it might transform us? When do we dismiss others because of what they look like on the surface, without welcoming them in?

3 A hardened forehead but receptive heart

Ezekiel 3:4–15

Ezekiel's magnificent first vision continues to unfold and the prophet is introduced to those to whom he will speak. Once again we are being prepared for the unrelenting harshness of the book that is to follow. These might be Ezekiel's own people, speaking his language, but they are those with 'a hard forehead and a stubborn heart' (v. 7). God's response is to harden the prophet's forehead 'like the hardest stone, harder than flint' (v. 9). Indeed, scholars remind us that his very name, Ezekiel, means 'God hardens/strengthens'. The people may be 'hard of forehead' but in this prophet it seems they have met their match.

We have been encouraged to read beyond the surface level of this scroll, however, and scholars call our attention to an unspoken but vital aspect of the passage. The people are not only hard of forehead, they are also stubborn of heart—yet the prophet is not told once that his heart will be hardened or made stubborn. Quite the opposite: he is to keep his heart open and receptive, ready to respond: 'all the words that I shall speak to you, receive in your heart' (v. 10). Once again, the prophet is offered as a model for us all.

There will be times when we need to be thickskinned, perhaps even calling on God to 'harden our forehead' as we are confronted with the need to say or do difficult things. At such moments, Ezekiel reminds us that, even in facing the most stubborn, hardhearted people, our hearts must never become tough or hardened. Instead, we must take the risk of holding within us a vulnerable 'heart of flesh' (a theme to which we shall return presently), which has the inherent capacity to be wounded. Even the one whose very name is 'God hardens' must keep his heart open and ready to receive from God.

4 The 'silent' prophet

Ezekiel 3:22–27

The first vision is drawing to a close but there is one further aspect of his prophetic ministry that the prophet is to discover. Ezekiel is to be silent, with his tongue clinging to the roof of his mouth, until God commands otherwise (v. 26). Scholars have struggled with this passage, aware that, according to 33:22, the prophet's mouth is explicitly opened around seven years later, following the fall of Jerusalem in 587BC ('so my mouth was opened, and I was no longer unable to speak'). If Ezekiel is to be silent, then how is it that he spends much of these seven years—and the intervening chapters of the book—proclaiming God's word? Indeed, Ezekiel shows himself to have an extraordinary capacity endlessly to stream forth words, with his incessant repetitions and details. Some have suggested that God simply removes the prophet's dumbness whenever he wishes him to prophesy in his name. Yet most believe that 33:22, combined with other passages that allude to the prophet's silence being lifted only after the destruction of Jerusalem (24:27, 29:21), does not encourage such a reading.

Robert Wilson has suggested an intriguing solution to the conundrum, focusing on the nuances of what God commands in verse 26. While the NRSV reads, 'you shall be… unable to reprove them' (with other translations similar), he suggests that a better translation of the phrase forbids the prophet from acting as 'legal mediator' in the dispute between God and the people. In other words, the prophet is banned from mediating on behalf of the people, from interceding for them or presenting their side of the story. The time for such arbitration is over. The people are given the choice either to hear or not to hear (v. 27), but no opportunity for dialogue. Yet again, we are warned of the dreadful words and judgment that are to come.

This is a troubling passage in a troubling book, but it gives us pause for thought. Our tongue does not cling to the roof of our mouth in our relationship with God; nor have we been banned from acting as mediator or intercessor on behalf of the people. This is a passage that witnesses forcefully to the privilege, gift and power of intercessory prayer—presenting us with a vision of a God who will indeed listen when we pray and who will respond to our mediation. For whom, then, will we pray?

5 Symbolic actions

Ezekiel 4:1–3

Ezekiel's first vision is over and his ministry begins. It is striking that it begins with a string of symbolic actions, a hallmark of this prophetic theologian. Scholars have been fascinated with the immense power of such symbolic actions to communicate God's message beyond words. The first example, in today's passage, gives us a taste of their force.

The prophet is commanded to draw Jerusalem on a brick, then build a siege against it, with miniature ramp, camps and battering rams. This is not child's play in 597BC, around ten years before the dreadful event will actually take place. To the traumatized exiles, far from home in Babylon, the sight of the city for which they long being put under siege would have been deeply distressing. The message that this sight holds is even bleaker. The prophet is responding to that crucial question: where is God in exile, siege and destruction? The answer can be found in the symbol of his own face, which becomes the face of God. This face is turned towards the city; it is watching. Yet there is an iron wall between God and the people: Jerusalem will come under siege and God will watch—indeed, it is only he who can 'let it be in a state of siege' (v. 3)—yet God will not intervene. The time for second chances is over. We are reminded of the silence forced upon the prophet, forbidden to intercede for his people (3:26) The destruction of Jerusalem is inevitable.

These verses confront us with a dreadful image, not of the absence of God but of the presence of a God who, for reasons beyond our understanding, will no longer be moved to pity. At the same time, it is striking that an 'iron wall' must be placed between God and his people to prevent God from responding. This is a powerful witness to God's overwhelming desire to respond to us when we cry out, encouraging us to do so.

Through symbolic actions, the prophet communicates his imperative messages visually and forcefully. We are reminded that the way in which we act communicates something about God, whether we wish it to or not. What messages are we conveying to friends, family and strangers as we go about our everyday life? What messages do we and our congregation convey about God to those worshipping at or visiting our churches?

6 Defilement of the temple

Ezekiel 8

It is time for Ezekiel's second vision, for which he is graphically grasped by his hair and wrenched into the heavens, to be transported back to Jerusalem. At last, the prophet sees the temple he has longed for, yet it is changed; and throughout the chapter we can sense his horror at what is taking place there. Neither the divine voice nor the prophet-priest can bear to mention the name of the image that has been placed in God's very presence: it is 'the image of jealousy' (v. 3). Even worse are the secretive practices of the elders, sanctifying with incense the 'disgusting things' (v. 10), which are forbidden even as food in Leviticus 11:10–42. Worse again are the women who have adopted the practices of the death-

and-resurrection cult of Tammuz (v. 14), and not even properly—they are performing their lamentations at the wrong time of year! The prophet's horrified description climaxes with the sight of men prostrating to the sun and, in so doing, unfathomably turning their backs to the glory of God. The temple is being most terribly defiled.

Key within this passage is the reason given for such indescribable behaviour: 'The Lord does not see us, the Lord has forsaken the land' (v. 12; see also 9:9). Jerusalem's beleaguered people believe that God has departed from them and so have sought replacements. The dreadful irony is that the glory of God is actually present, 'like the vision that I had seen in the valley' (v. 4). The very glory that rendered the prophet stunned and struggling for words in Ezekiel 1 is there, yet the people are blind to it. The tragedy is that their response is itself alienating God from the temple, which is becoming so defiled that his glory cannot bear to remain present. In the following chapters, God's glory will gather to leave, finally crossing the threshold in 10:18. Jerusalem's people have created for themselves their own greatest fear.

Ezekiel 8 provokes us to reflect on a number of issues. First, are there any areas in our lives where we are creating for ourselves our own greatest fear? How might we gain courage to stop ourselves from doing this? Second, to what or whom do we turn as replacements for God in our lives? Ezekiel reminds us that God is always present, even when we are numb or blind to that presence. Third, do we know anyone who is behaving inappropriately because they feel unseen? How might we treat this person as someone who is living in the light and love of God? Such treatment can be transformative.

Guidelines

In these first pages of Ezekiel, this remarkable prophetic theologian has confronted us with a tremendous vision of a God who is always present, even when we are blind to that presence or far from our places of usual encounter. This God is not limited to the boundaries that we would like safely to set for ourselves, whether theological, cultural or geographical, and God's glory will always unsettle us. A number of challenges have emerged from our reading this week. Among them are the following questions.

- Are we ready to perceive God in the most unexpected of places and alongside the most unlikely of people?
- When do we keep God's challenge to us at arm's length, assuming that we know its content, and not allowing it deep within us where it might transform us?
- Do we have the courage to remain vulnerable to God, even in situations where we must be thickskinned?
- What messages are we communicating about God through the way we act in our everyday life?
- Do we truly believe in the powerful role of intercession and are we putting this into practice in our daily lives?
- With what or whom do we replace God when life becomes difficult? Are we ready to give up this replacement?
- Do we know people who are behaving inappropriately because they feel that God is absent? How might we treat them as people who live in the light and love of God?

Reflect on the challenges that have struck home for you through Ezekiel so far, whether from within these notes or beyond, considering how you might respond to them, practically, positively and prayerfully.

1 A heart of flesh

Ezekiel 11:14–21

Many are astonished by this note of hope sounded within the desolation of Ezekiel 1—24. In these verses we are presented with two remarkable images. First, God speaks of himself as having been (literally) 'a little sanctuary' to the exiles (v. 16). For this priestly lover of the temple, this is extraordinary language. Scholars are divided: does 'little' mean 'for a little while' or 'to some extent' or is it a reference to size? Most agree that Ezekiel is struggling to articulate a tension between the precious sufficiency of God's presence in exile and the enduring priority of the temple as a place of encounter between God and his people. We might ask ourselves when we have had fleeting glimpses of God in unexpected places, and where is the enduring place of encounter with God for us?

It is the second image that has really caught imaginations through the centuries, however, as the people are promised a 'heart of flesh' (v. 19). The stoneheartedness of the people is about to be transformed. This passage is striking for two reasons. First, the initiative for the transformation is with God. Later, in 18:31, the people will be challenged to 'get yourselves a new heart'; here, however, the emphasis is on God's role in this saving work. As in the New Testament, we see within Ezekiel a tension between grace and works, between God's initiative and our own. At this point in the book, when the focus is on the appalling state of the people, we are perhaps relieved that the initiative for bringing about this new 'heart of flesh' within the people lies with God. Second, we are reminded of the prophet's commission in 3:4–15, where his forehead was hardened but he was commanded to keep his heart receptive to God's word. The people are also called to have this receptive heart, however vulnerable it might make them at this traumatic time of exile. We are provoked to ask: what in our hearts is as stubborn as stone? Are we prepared for God to remove it, giving us in its place a vulnerable, receptive heart of flesh?

The unexpected hope and beauty of this passage within the otherwise bleak words of Ezekiel 1—24 (coupled with its later echo in 36:26, where it more naturally belongs), have led many to believe that the words have been edited into this early stage of the book by later theologians, keen to remind us that this challenging book's goal is restoration and wholeness. The deft editing encourages us to consider when we can sound such a note of hope for those going through difficult periods, bringing them perspective and a glimpse of life beyond their present situation.

2 The useless vine

Ezekiel 15

We might be grateful for the oasis of hope we found in chapter 11, as we are about to enter the darkest part of the book. Here we encounter one of Ezekiel's famous word-pictures, as the prophet takes the traditional Judean symbol of the vine and deliberately distorts it to tremendous impact. In a culture where the vine is a plant of great worth, the prophet asks if this precious plant is indeed more valuable than any other timber, in a string of damning questions. (1) Can its wood be used to make anything? (2) Is it any good for hanging things from? (3) Is it useful for fuel and does burning make it any better? The answer to all of these questions is 'no'. The inhabitants of Jerusalem are compared to this vine—beyond any possible use or value.

Ezekiel 15 is not the only passage to turn the symbol of the vine inside out in this way. In Hosea 10:1, the 'luxuriant vine' can also be translated as 'empty vine'; in Jeremiah 2:21, the 'choice vine, from the purest stock' becomes 'wild'; in Isaiah 5:1–7, the 'choice vines' again become 'wild grapes' or even 'stinking weeds'. Yet Ezekiel, typically, goes further, not suggesting that the people are a beautiful vine gone bad, but insisting that this vine has never been any use for anything! Note how the passage neglects to mention that this vine might once have borne fruit, for instance—one of the main reasons why vines are treasured. This utterly pessimistic perspective is typical of Ezekiel. Indeed, we shall find that this book is willing even to rewrite history to force home its point that the people deserve no affection from God: they are as worthless and useless to God as a charred vine branch. This is chilling language, and those of us who are familiar with the story of God's love for his people might find ourselves wishing to interject.

Ezekiel 15 raises challenging questions for us about how we treat our past. When life is not going well, do we look back on our story with pessimistic eyes, seeing only what has been difficult or negative? When we feel abandoned, do we write God out of our story, as if we have never sensed God's action and presence within our lives? It might be tempting to do this for rhetorical impact, yet the witness of the other prophets suggests that it is not the only way to respond to difficult periods. It is equally possible to remember the ways in which God has worked in our lives in the past, even when God seems absent in the present moment.

3 Violence

Ezekiel 16:1–43

Ezekiel 16 is notorious for its deeply uncomfortable reading. Within this troubling narrative, we meet Jerusalem as a tiny, abandoned, female baby, who is adopted and then married by God. Provoking her husband's fury through her repeated 'prostitutions', she is stripped, beaten, humiliated and finally killed by the mob set on her by her husband. Scholars experience this narrative as difficult on multiple levels, troubled by its extreme physical violence (v. 40), its explicit sexual language, which is even more graphic in Hebrew ('your juice was poured out and your nakedness bared', v. 36), its obsession with female blood, whether through birth, menstruation or violence (vv. 6, 9, 22, 36, 38), and the utter silence of the beaten female figure. Particularly disquieting are the echoes of cycles of domestic abuse, where, after a period of extreme violence, the husband is 'calm, and will be angry no longer' (v. 42). This is one of the few passages excluded from both Jewish and Christian lectionaries and we might understand why many avoid it.

It is nevertheless vital that we recognize the presence of this narrative within the pages of sacred scripture. This is the book that began with the model of the prophet swallowing the scroll, even when it was covered with 'lamentation, mourning and woe', and finding it in his mouth, beyond that surface level, as 'sweet as honey' (3:3). A common scholarly response to Ezekiel 16 is to 'resistant read' Jerusalem as a woman actively choosing to live as a 'prostitute' in a businesslike manner, modelling herself on her teacher, God, who similarly gave a stranger presents (vv. 10–14) and entered into a sexual relationship with her (v. 8). Through such a reading, scholars argue, a sense of control is returned to the battered female. On entering parish life and encountering real-life women who had been forced into prostitution or experienced domestic violence, however, the inadequacy of such an approach became starkly apparent to me. To 'resist' the stories of such women or to 'play' with them in any way, even out of a desire to 'redeem' them, is utterly inappropriate.

Ezekiel 16 remains a disturbing passage, whose presence challenges us to reflect on our ability to listen to troubling stories. When we listen to the stories of others, do we blinker ourselves to the violence or difficulties that might be present, focusing only on that which we wish to hear? Do we continually search for easy resolution where there is pain or anger, or are we prepared to listen even when it becomes uncomfortable, neither striving to lessen what is dreadful nor seeking to move too quickly towards answers? Ezekiel 16 challenges us to develop our listening skills.

4 Taking responsibility

Ezekiel 18:1–4, 30–32

This crucial passage within Ezekiel opens with what appears to have been a popular proverb among the exiles (cf. Jeremiah 31:29), promoting the belief that they are suffering due to the actions of their parents. Immediately and forcefully it is refuted: 'no more shall it be used by you' (v. 3). In the past, this rejection has been understood to reflect the beginning of a movement from a corporate understanding of the people of God towards a perception of the individual's relationship with God. Recent scholarship, however, suggests that this passage is about something quite different and far more challenging for us.

Instead of ushering in a new theology of the individual (an anachronistic concept), most now believe that Ezekiel 18 is concerned with countering the fatalism of those who believe that they have no power over the situation in which they find themselves, who see life as an unalterable path mapped out before them, for which they have no responsibility. The prophet Ezekiel will have none of this. The downside is that the people need to come to terms with the part that they have played in their exile from the land. The upside is the sense of hope and promise that comes with this recognition, climaxing in verses 30–32, where the people are urged to 'get yourselves a new heart and a new spirit!' The contrast with the earlier promise that God himself will 'remove the heart of stone from their flesh and give them a heart of flesh' (11:19) could not be greater. Here the emphasis in that tension between works and grace is emphatically on the works of the people. They have control over their own destiny, and the passage ends with the clarion call: 'Why will you die, O house of Israel... Turn, then, and live!'

We are provoked to ask ourselves what we are doing to 'get ourselves a new heart and spirit'. Within the context of the book as a whole, such efforts must clearly be understood ultimately to be reliant on God's saving action. Nevertheless, Ezekiel 18 shows us that God desires some initiative on our part. What single change to our life could we make today so that we might become part of God's work within us, transforming our stubborn heart of stone to a vulnerable heart of flesh?

5 Rewriting history

We have experienced this prophet's willingness to revise history in the story of the vine (ch. 15). Here we witness a comprehensive rewriting of the story of God's people, and it is an disconcerting one. Scholars agree that this is the most radical revisioning of tradition among Old Testament historical writings, and its thrust is wholly negative. Within Ezekiel, Israel's history becomes a chilling account of disobedience, rebellion and profanation, with little or no hope present. From the birth of the nation in the exodus to the present day, God has been seeking to 'pour out my wrath upon them and spend my anger against them' (vv. 8, 13, 21, 33–34).

Within Ezekiel's new history, we experience the full force of this book's 'radical theocentricity'. All is done 'for the sake of my name' (vv. 9, 14, 22, 44), not for the people's sake. Indeed, so committed is the prophet to showing God's total control that he even portrays God as having deliberately given the people 'statutes that were not good and ordinances by which they could not live' in an attempt to 'horrify them' (vv. 25–26). It seems as if this is the only way the prophet can conceive that the people's rebellion might have reached such heights: God was willing it among them.

Ezekiel is a book of sharp extremes and we must remember that counterbalancing Ezekiel 20's emphasis on God as wholly responsible for (indeed, ruthlessly bent on) the people's punishment through exile is the equally clear emphasis on the responsibility of the people that we encountered just two chapters earlier in Ezekiel 18. At the same time, we are also perhaps warned of the shadow side of a one-dimensional theology where God is portrayed as in control of all things and where people have no active part to play in shaping history. We might ask ourselves, what is the 'shadow side' of our own theology? Are we conscious of it and its potential implications for others?

Perhaps most striking about Ezekiel 20 for our purposes, however, is the cyclical nature of the history it presents. Lyle Eslinger calls attention to repeating 'panels' throughout this narrative, as the history repeatedly revolves through (1) God's actions, (2) covenant agreement, (3) rebellion, (4) divine wrath and (5) the sake of God's name. It is in part the cyclical nature of this history, from which the people appear unable to break free, that is so troubling. In what ways are we caught up in unhealthy cyclical patterns in our lives? How can we spot such cycles and seek to break free from them?

6 Child abuse

Ezekiel 23:1–35

In Ezekiel 23 we are confronted with one of the most disturbing narratives in the Bible. As troubling as chapter 16 for its graphic language and violence against female figures and as disconcerting as chapter 20 for its negative revisioning of the story of Israel and Judah, Ezekiel 20 adds to this already disquieting combination echoes of child abuse. We meet the young sisters Oholah (Israel) and Oholibah (Judah) as girls engaging in 'prostitution' in Egypt (v. 3) and follow their story from that point to their violent deaths. Many call attention to the sisters' young age at the beginning of this narrative and the passive nature of their sexual experience, which is explicitly in 'their youth': there their 'breasts were squeezed and their virgin nipples pressed'. Van Dijk-Hemmes has insisted that instead of 'prostitution', such an experience should be named as child abuse: 'They were sexually abused in Egypt, in their youth they were sexually abused.' This call to rename the girls' experience gains strong validity when we remember that this passage recalls the Hebrews' time of slavery in Egypt, for which 'abuse' seems far more appropriate language than voluntary 'prostitution'.

Oholah and Oholibah never manage to shake off the consequences of their dreadful treatment in Egypt. Throughout the narrative, their increasing 'prostitutions' and 'lust' are understood to be grounded in the experience of their youth (vv. 8, 19, 21, 27). Indeed, the sisters are presented as being caught up in a powerful cycle, or gathering spiral, from which they appear powerless to escape. It began with their sexual experience in Egypt and now relentlessly draws the sisters towards their inevitable destruction.

This is a deeply disturbing text. Countless scholars alert us to the echoes of the stories of children who have experienced sexual abuse and felt marked for life, perhaps even unable to escape from its implications for them. We are particularly reminded of those who have suffered from such abuse within the Church and whose experience has been misnamed or covered over. This is an opportunity to pray for those people and to ask God's forgiveness for the Church and the way it has often reacted. In addition, we are perhaps challenged to look at our own lives and to reflect on whether there are events from the past that have bound us and from whose implications we feel we cannot escape. We are perhaps advised to remember, at this darkest point in a book of dreadful extremes, that glimpse of hope wisely offered by those theologians in chapter 11 of the new heart of flesh and promise of renewal that is about to break forth within Ezekiel.

Guidelines

This week has confronted us with some of the most challenging and unsettling parts of Ezekiel, as the prophetic theologian has wrestled to reveal the presence of God in the darkness of exile. Encountering these disquieting narratives will have left us with a number of questions about ourselves and our daily lives. Some of them might include the following.

- What in our hearts is as stubborn as stone? Are we prepared for God to remove this hardheartedness, giving us instead a vulnerable heart of flesh?
- What we are changing within our lives in order to 'get ourselves a new heart and spirit'?
- How do we remember our past, particularly when life is not going well? Do we look back with pessimistic eyes, writing God out of our story?
- What is the 'shadow side' of our theology? Are we conscious of it and its potential implications for others?
- How developed are our listening skills? Do we have the ability truly to listen to the stories of others, even when they are challenging or unsettling for us?
- Are we caught up in any unhealthy cycles within our life or are there events in our past that bind us? How might we break free from these cycles, with God's help?

Let us take time to reflect on these and other issues that have arisen for us this week, bringing them before the God of all power and glory.

1 Eliminating the 'other'

Ezekiel 26:1—28:19

The tide is preparing to change within Ezekiel towards restoration. Yet before the prophet will finally begin to offer hope to the scattered exiles, he turns his fury towards the foreign nations in chapters 25—32, whom he accuses of glorifying themselves over the dreadful fate of the Judeans. Babylon, Tyre, Ammon, Moab, Edom, Philistia, Egypt, Ethiopia, Put, Lud, Arabia, Libya and Sidon, among others, fall subject to the tirade of this hardened prophet. The lamentation in 32:1–16 over Pharaoh, king of that ancient nation Egypt, provides a taste of the content and language involved.

Scholars debate whether passages such as this should be considered alongside the judgment oracles of chapters 1—24 or alongside the hope and restoration oracles of chapters 33—48. Some consider the oracles against the nations to be words of hope to the Judean exiles, as God turns his wrath away from them and towards the nations. Others call attention to their violence and negativity, stressing that they present us with as much of a challenge as the judgment oracles addressed to Judah and Jerusalem. We are perhaps reminded of how quickly we can turn to eliminate or scapegoat the 'other' when under pressure. When do we, in our own lives, redirect our anger and negativity at others in order to make ourselves feel better? How often do we seek to find confidence for ourselves or those we love by being critical of the weaknesses of others, particularly those who are different from us, rather than in being assured of the strengths given to us by God?

2 Shepherd of the sheep

Ezekiel 34:1–22

At last, hope is about to dawn in Ezekiel. Within the rest of this book we will see God acting powerfully to reverse those factors that brought about the defilement and exile of the people. It is striking that God begins by tackling Judah's leadership, drawing on the popular ancient Near Eastern metaphor of shepherd for those who rule (which is later to become so strongly influential in the parables and teachings of Jesus). Here in Ezekiel 34, those shepherds who were entrusted with pasturing the people of God have failed in their role. They will thus be removed from their office and God himself will act as shepherd: there is now to be a direct relationship between God and his people (vv. 15–16). In a verse of great beauty, which we might hardly recognize in this book that until now has been so negative, God promises himself to seek the lost, bring back the strayed, bind the injured and strengthen the weak.

The shepherds in this passage remain unnamed. Many scholars believe that this omission is deliberate, meaning that all with leadership responsibilities in any area are being addressed. In what places do we have responsibility to strengthen, heal, bind wounds, gather the strayed and seek the lost? Are we attending to these responsibilities, responding to God's call to us, or are we simply looking to our own needs and hoping for them to be fulfilled (v. 10)?

In verses 20–22, God moves from his focus on the shepherds to turn his gaze also to the sheep. They may have had inappropriate and in-effective shepherds, but they remain accountable for their actions: in the eyes of God, pushing out the weaker sheep and scattering them abroad is utterly unacceptable. We are reminded that even when we do not hold a position of leadership, we are still charged by God with watching out for the weak. Who are the vulnerable in our communities and how are we taking care to see that they are not being marginalized, isolated and scattered?

3 The valley of dry bones

Ezekiel 37:1–14

The prophet is transported once again by the Lord to a valley 'full' of bones. The sheer scale of the horror is repeatedly underscored: there are 'very many' of them and they are 'very dry' (v. 2). Confronted with this sight of utter desolation, we might wonder what message Ezekiel expects to be forced to convey—more words of condemnation over the already devastated people? When asked, 'Can these bones live?' the shaken prophet can only reply, 'O Lord God, you know' (v. 3), waiting in trepidation to hear the crucial response. It is astonishing, then, that when God speaks it is to say that breath will be breathed and these dry bones shall live. Resonances with the Lord God gently breathing life into the first man (Genesis 2:7) reverberate: even the same verb, 'to breathe', is used, as the possibilities of new creation are breathed into this remarkable book. The only difference is that, in Ezekiel, the four winds themselves are to be summoned, so numerous is the 'vast multitude' to be revived and recreated.

This inspirational vision is perhaps the most famous passage in the whole of Ezekiel, immortalized within popular culture in the African spiritual, 'Dem bones'. Born among those who found themselves captive in a foreign land, estranged from all that was familiar, this spiritual witnesses to a depth of empathy for the hopes and desires of exiles that few can match. It is striking, then, that 'Dem bones' focuses so closely on verse 7, in which the bones come together with a rattling sound: 'Your toe bone connected to your foot bone, your foot bone connected to your ankle bone, your ankle bone connected to your leg bone.'

This extraordinary focus on connections is deeply moving in the context of a people who have been estranged from their homeland, their extended families and even their immediate families, as brothers and sisters, husbands and wives, parents and children were separated from each other through the slave trade. The hope, desire and belief, in such dark circumstances, that such connections might nevertheless be remade through God's activity is a powerful challenge to us. We live in a society where many are estranged: married couples, extended families, faith communities, cultural groups, churches across denominations, rich and poor, different generations. Can we also catch a glimpse of the prophet's vision of a valley where even the driest, most scattered bones can be reconnected and brought to life? Perhaps most importantly, how, like the prophesying prophet, might we become part of bringing about this reconnection in our immediate situation?

4 A new temple

Ezekiel 40:1–16; 44:4–9

The closing nine chapters present us with Ezekiel's final vision. In the first vision, the prophet unexpectedly encountered God in exile (ch. 1); in the second, he was taken on a tour of the defiled temple and watched the glory of the Lord depart in repulsion (ch. 8). Here in chapters 40—49, Ezekiel is taken on a second tour of the temple, newly purified and restored, during which the glory of the Lord will return to stun the prophet once again (43:1–5; 44:3).

Much of the vision consists of detailed descriptions and measurements, illustrated by the first passage provided. Scholars have devalued these chapters in the past, considering them to be overly repetitive and of little interest. Indeed, it was not uncommon to assume these closing passages to be later additions, unworthy of our attention. Current scholarship has generally moved to restore interest in Ezekiel's final vision, however, emphasizing the vitality of the temple for this prophetic priest, even portraying these chapters as the climax of the book. Such responses call attention to the human tendency to see God working only in those things that are comfortable for us, challenging us to broaden our understanding of where God's activity might be found. Clearly the restoration of the temple is a source of great joy within Ezekiel, and the prophet lovingly revels in the detail.

Ezekiel's final vision is not wholly positive, however. Some call attention to the absence of the female personification of the restored temple, which is never once called 'Jerusalem', in stark contrast to chapter 16. Others highlight the troubling exclusion of foreigners in 44:4–9. Much in these nine chapters is concerned with safeguarding the temple from any potential future defilement. It seems that, in the aftermath of the trauma of exile, to continue to personify the temple as a female and to admit foreign people who might introduce alternative forms of worship (cf. Ezekiel 8) is too much of a risk for this prophetic theologian. Scholars note the stark contrast between this response to the exile and that of Isaiah 40—55, which promotes the personification of the redeemed Zion as a female (49:14–23; 52:1–10; 54:1–8 and so on), uses female imagery to describe God (42:14; 49:14–15; cf. 66:13) and holds Israel up as a 'light to the nations' (49:6). We are challenged to reflect on how we respond when our theology and comfortable forms of worship have been unsettled. Do we seek to introduce more boundaries and safeguards to prevent it from happening again or do we take the opportunity to open up our worship and conceptions of God in new ways?

5 Treading the saltmarshes

Ezekiel 47

Within the prophet's final vision comes this glorious passage where the waters of life wash through the newly restored temple and over the astonished prophet, flowing ever onwards to bring new life even to the Dead Sea, as Engedi to En-eglaim are refreshed. The temple may be renewed but God is still greater than its most beautiful limits, still moving beyond any boundaries that we might create. Resonances with Eden's rivers in Genesis 2:10–14 once again remind us of the new creation that is being miraculously and wonderfully brought about. No wonder this passage inspired the great vision of Revelation 22:1–2, where the water of life flowing 'from the throne of God and of the Lamb' waters the fruitful tree of life, whose leaves are 'for the healing of the nations'.

In the midst of this tribute to the life-giving power of God lies a verse often skipped over by lectionaries, perhaps anxious that it might bring a negative note to the vision: 'But its swamps and marshes will not become fresh; they are to be left for salt' (v. 11). We should not be afraid of this verse, for within it lies one of the great treasures of the passage. Salt in the ancient Near East was neither simply a condiment added for taste, nor a substance used to preserve, although it may well have been used for these purposes. Salt was essential for life, used as a fertilizer to bring precious sustainability to limited land and to purify pollutants. It is in this context that we should understand verse 11 and its vision for the marshes and swamps, left for the creation of salt.

In the Gospel of Matthew, Jesus tells us that our role as disciples is to be 'salt of the earth' (5:13). Ezekiel 47 reminds us that salt is crystallized not in the well-watered places of the world but in the salt marshes and swamps—what we might call the waste places, mess and mud of life. We are provoked to ask ourselves, in what ways does the living water of God flow through and around us and when are we in the salt marshes and swamps of life? Perhaps most importantly, how are we taking that salt to others, bringing sustenance, life and purification to them? As Luke 14:34–35 warns us, 'Salt is good; but if salt has lost its taste, how can its saltiness be restored? It is fit neither for the soil nor for the manure pile; they throw it away. Let anyone with ears to hear listen.'

6 'The Lord is there'

Ezekiel 48:30–35

The book of Ezekiel closes amid swarms of detail and attention to measurements, which continue to the very last verse of the book, even giving us the circumference of the holy city. Yet a short closing phrase ends the book in confidence. The name of that city will be not 'Jerusalem' (*yerushalayim*) any more, but *yahweh* shammah, 'The Lord is there'. Many are conscious of the deliberate wordplay on the abandoned name 'Jerusalem' to create a new identity for the city.

The name 'The Lord is there' provides a dramatic and fitting ending for this book, which opened with God being 'there' in Babylon with the exiles. Order and restoration have now fully returned, with the temple in place and God present, reigning permanently from his throne. This is the climax of Ezekiel's final vision for the temple: all those previous details, all that care and attention to details and measurements, would come to nothing without the presence of God, which shall be there 'from that time on'.

We are provoked to ask ourselves what we give our time and attention to in our daily lives. The tasks with which we are presented at home, work or church can involve significant attention to detail and commitment to focus. This is at times appropriate and necessary. In the end, however, we are reminded that the last word must always be 'The Lord is there'. Ezekiel—even with his extraordinary capacity for detail—reminds us that this is all that matters. We are called to let all things in our life become a temple to the Lord. These things cannot become a temple if God is not present: instead, they become empty, meaningless places where people do strange things in the dark (see 8:12). What tasks face us today? Let us take care to close each of them with the words 'the Lord is there'.

Guidelines

In reading Ezekiel, we have experienced the movement from desolation and a sense of judgment through to restoration and hope. Can we trace this movement within us in our own lives? Ezekiel remains a challenging book, even in the midst of its oracles of hope, with an immense capacity to unsettle us. Where has God been at work in us this week, preparing within us that new heart of flesh in place of our stubborn heart of stone?

We have been confronted with a number of issues this week, in addition to those personal reflections provoked by this extraordinary book.

- When do we redirect anger and negativity at others in order to feel better ourselves, highlighting the weaknesses of others rather than finding confidence in the strengths given to us by God?
- If we are leaders, are we attending to our responsibilities to strengthen, heal, bind wounds, gather the strayed and seek the lost? If we have no leadership responsibility, are we still careful to look out for the vulnerable in our society, taking care that they are not being marginalized or isolated?
- How can we become part of God's desire to bring about connectedness in a society where people live estranged in so many different ways?
- How do we respond when our theology or worship is unsettled? Do we introduce more rigid safeguards, preventing it from happening again, or do we take the opportunity to open up our worship and understanding of God in new ways?
- In what ways does the living water of God flow through and around us? When are we in the salt marshes and swamps of life? How are we taking that salt to others?
- Is our last thought in all that we do, amid all the planning and attention to detail, 'the Lord is there'?

Let us take time to consider what God is seeking to transform within our lives. How will we offer this up to him, with an open, vulnerable and receptive heart?

FURTHER READING

Lyle Eslinger, 'Ezekiel 20 and the Metaphor of Historical Teleology: Concepts of Biblical Theology', *JSOT* 81 (1998), pp. 93–125, esp. p. 99.

F. Van Dijk-Hemmes, 'The Metaphorization of Woman in Prophetic Speech: An Analysis of Ezekiel XXIII', in A. Brenner and F. van Dijk-Hemmes, *On Gendering Texts: Female and Male Voices in the Hebrew Bible,* Brill, 1993, pp. 167–76, especially p. 173.

Robert R. Wilson, 'An Interpretation of Ezekiel's Dumbness', *Vetus Testamentum*, 22:1 (January 1972), pp. 91–104.

ACTS 1—15

The book of Acts has a unique place in the New Testament. Indeed, some scholars argue that without Acts the New Testament would not exist at all, for it is only the book of Acts that allows the Gospels and the letters to hang together. Acts itself is the second part of two volumes by Luke (see Luke 1:1–4; Acts 1:1–2), so it is intended to continue the story from the Gospels into the life of the Church. At the same time, however, Acts depicts aspects of the life of Paul, Peter, James and John who, between them, have their names on almost every letter in the New Testament and the book of Revelation. Thus the letters can be 'located' within Acts, not necessarily in the sense of identifying when and where they were written but providing background on the characters who wrote them and the way they related to each other.

The historical accuracy of Acts has come under much scrutiny. A key point of controversy is between those who see Acts' depiction of fundamental harmony between the different apostles and leaders as truthful and those who see it as a later attempt to 'paper over the cracks'. However, its accuracy is difficult to assess, for there is little with which to compare it. As the only source for the early days in Jerusalem, for example, how can its accuracy be gauged? The exception is in the case of Paul, where Acts' portrait of Paul can be compared to the picture Paul gives of himself in his letters. Unsurprisingly, some see the differences as natural given different texts written by different people at different times from different perspectives, while others identity differences so great as to challenge Acts' accuracy (for example, over the relationship between the events surrounding Paul in Acts 9—15 and Galatians 1—2).

Most scholars date Acts to between AD75 and 90—after the Gospel of Luke, which itself is placed after the destruction of the temple in AD70, but before Paul's letters started to be collected (for there is no mention of them in Acts). Traditionally, its author is seen as travelling with Paul for parts of the journeys depicted (notice the word 'they' in 16:6–10 changing to 'we' in 16:11 onwards). This view is challenged by those who feel that it is not accurate enough about Paul to have been written by his companion.

There are a number of themes in Acts to look out for. Continuity and discontinuity—between Judaism and the followers of Jesus—are at the heart of the book. This issue touches on interfaith relationships today. It also speaks to the sense of continuity and discontinuity experienced in the Church today, as we move from 'Christendom' to a time when Christianity is a misunderstood minority part of society—rather like it is in Acts. Mission is the lifeblood of Acts in a way that it is not in the letters (which generally focus on the Church, not the world outside). Acts forces us to think about whether we are prepared to change the way in which we 'do church' for the sake of the outsiders, or whether they are welcome only if they do things our way. Acts also presents us with confident use of the Old Testament, often neglected by the Church today, and speaks clearly of the role of the Spirit.

Acts is a long, rich book, so we will look at the first half in this issue of *Guidelines* and complete it next time. Where the Bible is quoted, the English translation has been taken from the New International Version.

1 The story continues

Acts 1

This first chapter provides a bridge between the Gospels focused on Jesus' actions and the Acts *of the apostles*. It begins with Jesus teaching his disciples after the resurrection, but by its end we are set for Pentecost and the 'birth' of the Church.

As in all transitions, there is both continuity and discontinuity. Continuity is stressed in the opening words. The Gospel was about what Jesus began to do; Acts will tell the story of what Jesus continued to do. There is a difference, of course. He is no longer physically present: he has gone 'into heaven' (v. 11). In his place there will be God's own Spirit (vv. 4, 8): the logic here is close to John's description of the Spirit as 'another Counsellor' in some way replacing Jesus (John 14:15–21, 25–27; 16:5–15).

Many details also emphasize continuity. Jesus speaks about the 'kingdom of God' (v. 3); his message has the same focus as it did before his death and resurrection (e.g. Luke 4:43). This was what the disciples were originally sent to proclaim (Luke 9:1–2) and, although the phrase is rare in Acts, right at the end we see Paul preaching the same message (28:31). Mention of the Mount of Olives (v. 12) and two angels asking why they are standing looking (v. 11) link directly back to Gethsemane and the resurrection (Luke 22:39–53; 24:4–5). Judas' replacement (vv. 21–22) also stresses continuity: the newly appointed apostle needs to be a witness of the resurrection but also of Jesus' whole ministry. Just as Jesus chose the original Twelve (Luke 6:13–16), he chooses the replacement (v. 24).

The question of Judas reveals an approach to understanding events that is pursued throughout Acts (and introduced on the Emmaus road, Luke 24:13–35). What happened with Judas is surprising but, in retrospect, we can see that it fulfilled scripture (v. 20). Thus it does not challenge the idea that God is in control; it only highlights our need for humility and openness to the fact that God's plan may be different from our expectations.

There is one noticeable discontinuity. In the Gospel the Twelve are called 'disciples' or 'learners'; now they are 'apostles' (which means 'envoys' or 'messengers'). Their role is no longer focused on learning but on being sent out to witness (vv. 8, 22).

Continuity and discontinuity are at the heart of the book of Acts. As Jesus continues to work, what should remain the same and what should change? The same question is at the heart of most issues in the Church today, particularly as we think of our mission and our calling to be witnesses.

2 Pentecost

Acts 2:1–41

This account of the receipt of the Spirit sets up many of the themes that run throughout Acts. The Spirit himself is crucial: nothing important happens throughout the rest of Acts apart from the Spirit. We also have the pattern of a dramatic event giving rise to an explanation: people's curiosity is provoked before the gospel is proclaimed.

The receipt of the Spirit brings into being a new community. Pentecost originally celebrated the time when God gave the law at Mount Sinai in earthquake and fire and formed a new nation from the twelve tribes by giving them the law to guide them (Exodus 19—20). Now, at a new

Pentecost, God revealed in wind and fire forms a new (or renewed) 'nation', based around the twelve apostles, giving them the Spirit as their guide. This marks out the beginning of a new and final period of history (the 'last days').

The new 'nation' gathers together Jews scattered across the world. Symbolically we see the reversal of the exile, the long-promised gathering of the people of Israel from every corner of the world (e.g. Isaiah 43:5–6), and even a reversal of the divisions between the nations at the tower of Babel (Genesis 11:1–9). We also see a foretaste of the gospel going to the ends of the earth (1:8). The question of the relationship between this new community and the existing Jewish community, unanswered here, reverberates throughout the rest of the book.

We find similar long speeches punctuating the rest of Acts—similar not just in form but in their approach, connecting the scriptures with Jesus' death and resurrection and with the experience or memory of the hearers, and concluding with a call for urgent action and the offer of forgiveness or salvation. While containing harsh words (see, for example, v. 36), the overall thrust of the speech is good news: God has acted; salvation is available to all who call (vv. 21, 38–40), young and old, rich and poor, male and female (vv. 17–18, 39).

This message of equality fits well with our society today, but the presentation of a 'metanarrative' (that is, an overall universal story within which we and the events we see find their place) fits less well. The Church as a place uniting different cultures, or even different generations, is an aspiration rarely fulfilled.

3 The believers' community

Acts 2:42–47; 4:32–37

For ease, we bring together in this reading the two passages in the early chapters of Acts depicting the believers' community. These two passages have the effect of giving balance in chapters 2—5: the dramatic events that inevitably take the lion's share of the narrative need to be seen within the overall framework of the community's ongoing life.

The lives of those who were baptized and brought into this new community are transformed. The community is led by the apostles, who not only witness with great power and do miraculous signs, but are also responsible for the practical organization of the community. In their teaching and performing of miracles, and in their more general leadership of the community and care for those with practical needs, they continue the work of Jesus. The community is focused on God in prayer and praise and through meeting in the temple. It is also marked out by joy.

The community is united. This unity is expressed in general terms such as 'devoted... to the fellowship', 'were together' and 'one in heart and mind' (2:42, 44; 4:32) but is particularly manifest in the handling of possessions. The meaning of 'everything in common' (2:44) has been at the centre of much discussion, particularly given the clash between 'communism' and 'capitalism' in the last century (in which, ironically, communism tended to be married to atheism). However, such discussions about economic systems probably miss the point. Here, as is made clearer in 4:32–37, the focus is not ownership but the unity of the community; the meeting of needs, not a grand scheme for the reorganization of society. Private ownership continued (4:34, 37; 5:1, 4) but the underlying attitude was that possessions were held for the benefit of the whole community: 4:32 could be translated as 'Nobody claimed that their possessions were a private matter'. This is a challenge in our age, when talking about money is often the last taboo, but it is a necessary one, for 'where your treasure is, there your heart will be also' (Matthew 6:21).

The phrase 'they broke bread... and ate together' (2:46) is significant. In this, they seem to be continuing the practice of Jesus, who was known for having festive meals, anticipating the kingdom of God (Luke 5:27–35; 7:31–35; 14:15–24). However, it may also have a particular reference to the re-enactment or remembrance of the last meal that Jesus had with his disciples before his arrest (Luke 22:7–23). Later in Acts, 'break bread' seems to be used as a technical term for this ritual (20:7).

4 The healing of a disabled man

Acts 3

This story has similarities with Pentecost, in that the speech is occasioned by an event that draws a crowd. Peter and John do not set out to preach on the streets; rather, God's activity through them generates interest and questioning and thus an occasion to explain. The story also has similarities with some of Jesus' miracles: the community, together with the Spirit, is continuing the work that Jesus began.

The miracle causes difficulties because it is high-profile: the man had been disabled from birth and was well known for begging at the entrance to the temple, and was now, healed, very visible within it. The temple itself had been the focal point of Jesus' clash with the religious authorities: he had symbolically attacked it (Luke 19:45–46; 21:5–6; 23:44–46) and its ruling priests had arranged his death (Luke 22:66—23:24). Once again the temple is at the centre of the dispute over Jesus—appropriately, since it was at the heart of Jewish life. The scene is now set for further preaching from the apostles (the rest of chapter 3) and the negative response from the temple authorities (chapter 4).

Peter's speech is similar to that at Pentecost, though tying into the healing (vv. 12, 16) as opposed to the giving of the Spirit (2:14–21). The healing done in Jesus' name reinforces the point made by the resurrection (of which they are witnesses). God was with Jesus, and the authorities' opposition to Jesus (in some collective sense: note the temple setting) is in fact opposition to God. This can be overlooked, however; indeed, their complicity in Jesus' death is labelled as 'ignorance' (v. 17). Forgiveness, refreshment and blessing are now on offer (vv. 19, 26).

The mention of the 'prophet like Moses' (v. 22; see Deuteronomy 18:15–19) is more than just another 'messianic' prophecy. Allegiance to Moses defined the boundary of the community; the 'new Moses' will do the same (v. 23). The implication might be understated but is clear. Moses himself said that a prophet 'like him' would come, around whom the boundaries of God's people would be redefined: if Jews did not listen to him, they would be cut off from God's people. Peter identifies that 'prophet like Moses' with Jesus, which would mean that his fellow Jews will be 'cut off' if they do not listen to Jesus. The idea of a new community formed at Pentecost is developing a harder edge. God's purpose is to bless the Jews 'first' (v. 26) but the blessing is for 'all peoples' (v. 25). This passage raises difficult questions for Christian–Jewish relationships. The idea of God's community being redefined also challenges us today: where truly is the community of Jesus' followers to be found?

5 Arrest

Jesus' teaching created opposition, but when he acted in the temple it turned to violence (Luke 11:53–54; 19:45–48). So too for Peter and John, as Jesus continues to work through them. They are soon facing the same group who were instrumental in Jesus' death just a few months before (vv. 5–6; Luke 22:66). Now, full of the Spirit, Peter does not disown Jesus but speaks the words given him as Jesus had promised (Luke 21:12–15). The parallels and scriptural background are not lost on the believers (vv. 25–27).

The 'trial' focuses on the person and name of Jesus. The authorities attempt to separate the 'good deed' and the life of the community from this focus on Jesus: the apostles are not to speak in his name any more (v. 17). They cannot deny that good things have happened; they just don't want the connection with Jesus. Parallels can be seen with much in our own society: the good works of the church are welcomed but there is pressure to downplay the 'Jesus element'. Pious people doing good works are welcome; focus on Jesus is not.

The bravery of the apostles in choosing to 'follow God' is easy to underestimate. These same authorities had not long earlier arranged the gruesome, torturous death of Jesus. Opposing them was suicidal. (John's brother is indeed killed in Acts 12:2.) Equally important, though, is their identification of and resistance to the temptation being offered to them, to compromise over Jesus. They are clear: the rejected one is now the key; salvation is exclusively available in Jesus (vv. 11–12: notice how Peter argues that this claim for exclusivity is found within the very scriptures that his fellow Jews accept). Exclusivity is a difficult concept in our age— the stumbling block in all 'interfaith' dialogue is the Christian claim about Jesus—but here we see that the issues are not really new at all.

The community's response is to turn to God in prayer. Trusting in God's sovereignty, and encouraged by the fact that the scriptures show these negative events to be part of God's plan (just as for Jesus' death: Luke 24:18–27), they also recognize the temptation to be bullied or seduced. So they pray for boldness to continue and for God to continue to work through them despite the dangers that this work produces (vv. 29–30). How we react to setbacks is very revealing.

6 God at work

Soon Peter and John will be back in front of the authorities. Before that, however, we have the curious incident of Ananias and Sapphira.

This story alerts us to the fact that the community was not perfect (indeed, note that this passage follows on from the discussion of the community being 'one in heart and mind'). To understand it, we need to notice that the couple's sin was not that they kept their money; they had every right to do that. The sin was that they lied about it (v. 4). They could keep the money to themselves or they could give it to the community. What they could not do was pretend that they were giving it to the community when they were keeping it. Furthermore, the sin was serious because it was not in fact the community they were lying to but God. Put another way, God is present in this community (as opposed to being present in the temple, perhaps). How easily we set up expectations for ourselves and for others that we cannot keep; then, rather than admitting our shortcomings, we encourage hypocrisy and deception.

The picture of the community's impact in verses 12–16 is interesting, in that it highlights how the community was good news for those around it. Although God was in it and, in a sense, protecting it (vv. 1–11), and there was an amazing common life (2:42–47; 4:32–37), it was not focused in on itself. Nor even was it focused on winning converts, although God brought more people to believe. It was a blessing to those around it and seen positively by the people as a result.

The opposition grows once more. This time it is the whole group of the apostles who are arrested. God, however, is in control, as demonstrated by the miraculous release from prison (v. 19). The issue is the same as in the previous hearing: the name of Jesus. The apostles offer no compromise on this issue. Jesus was raised by God from the dead and is the source of forgiveness for Israel, and it is as his followers that they have received God's own Spirit. Gamaliel, in effect, follows this line of argument, accepting that the key question is whether Jesus (and, hence, his followers) was God's agent or not. 'Where is God?' and 'Who is speaking and acting for him?' are the key questions, though they are often left unasked.

Guidelines

These first five chapters of Acts raise many issues for us to ponder. A number are given below. Choose two or three to think and pray about.

• Acts talks of Jesus continuing to work now. Are you conscious that God at work today is the Jesus whose life and character we see in the Gospels? What difference does this make?

• The apostles seek to connect events in their day with the scriptures. We can be wary of this approach because of the way some people try to connect world events to details in the book of Revelation, for example. Leaving that aside, however, try to connect events in your life with parts of the scriptures. What scriptural patterns and principles can you see in your life?

• The Twelve were turned from disciples into apostles, from learners into messengers. Why do churches promote discipleship, not apostleship? Do you think more about being a learner or a messenger? Why?

• Does your church community unite cultures and ages? Does it reflect the age and racial make-up of the wider community? Look at your church council/body of elders. Are power and influence disproportionally held by one section of the community?

• Do you believe that money is a private matter?

• Does Jesus define your church community? Are you conscious of pressure to play down the name of Jesus? How do you react?

• Are there unreasonable, unnecessary expectations placed upon you by your church community or by yourself? Is there a danger that these will lead people into hypocrisy and deception?

• Is your church community seen as a blessing to the wider community?

1 Disputes

Acts 6

The community of believers now encompasses a range of cultures and backgrounds within Judaism: Galileans (the original group), Jerusalemites (the more recent converts), priests (despite the tension between Jesus and the temple, v. 7) and both Hebrew/Aramaic and Greek Jews (v. 1). Exactly what is meant by these last two terms is not clear: they could refer to the language spoken or, more generally, to Jews more or less influenced by Greek culture, but the distinction represents the key cultural and linguistic division within Judaism. It is not surprising that in Jerusalem the Greek Jews feel marginalized.

These cultural differences crystallize over a practical issue (just as issues of immigration are expressed in terms of access to housing, services and jobs; and varieties of Christianity are expressed through music, language and even dress). In a male-dominated society, widows are particularly vulnerable and need the support of a wider family or community. The believers have taken on this role: they are truly forming a new community with all its obligations. The problem is solved by a structural reorganization involving changes of roles and power. There is no suggestion that with a bit more goodwill, thoughtfulness or prayer it will all work out. The two 'services'—of the word and of the food distribution —are both necessary so leaders are appointed to take charge of each. It is noticeable that those who are responsible for this 'mundane' work still need to be 'full of the Spirit'. Indeed, Stephen, one of the chosen 'seven', is soon said to be preaching and doing great miracles (vv. 8–10).

Stephen then clashes with the wider Jewish community (verse 12 implies a broad cross-section). The accusation, said to be false, is that he speaks against the law and the temple. Nevertheless, there is a real clash underneath. For Stephen, the only issue is loyalty to Jesus, thus law and temple are secondary. For the wider community, any loyalty to Jesus must come second to the more general Jewish priority on law and temple (similar arguments are at the heart of Paul's trials in Acts 22—26, taking place 20 years later). By seeming to imply that law and temple are less important, Stephen presents a contrary view of what defines the people of God. Although Peter has already made similar implications (see, for example, 3:22–23, 4:12); on Stephen's lips the issue is clearly more controversial, perhaps because of his Greek background. Questions of community identity and loyalty to the shared history are often parti- cularly controversial. I am an Anglican, but if you ask what are the defining features of Anglicanism, you can quickly get contradictory views expressed very strongly.

2 Stephen's speech

Stephen retells the Jewish story from a particular perspective: which community—the emerging distinctive community of believers in Jesus or the wider community—is the true inheritor of God's promises? He focuses on the early history, prior to Sinai, for this supports his point that the temple and the law are not central to the Jewish story: they appear only at a later point. It is a story of promise, suffering and reversals (rather like Jesus' story).

The focal point is the question of obedience, and Stephen finds both sides within the Jewish story itself. Abraham obeyed God (vv. 3–4), while at other times other parts of the Jewish community have disobeyed (vv. 39–43) and created 'gods' of their own choosing. By speaking in this way, he locates the very argument that he is having with his fellow Jews within the scriptures themselves: there has always been disagreement and division within Judaism. The fact that the believers are a minority disagreeing with the wider community does not demonstrate that they are wrong or divergent; the Jewish story itself includes other cases where the minority were the ones obeying God, while the majority were following their own desires. The only thing that matters is making the choice to obey God (see 4:18–20; 5:38–39). More controversially, Stephen does not say, 'You are the inheritors of the Jewish story; we are starting a new thing here with Jesus.' Throughout, he appeals to the common Jewish heritage that he and his opponents share. His assertion is that the believers in Jesus are living out the role, found in the scriptures, of obedient Jews, while the wider community is living out the pattern of disobedience to God, found, for example, in the incident of the golden calf (v. 41; Exodus 32).

This argument might seem intolerant and unnecessarily aggressive to us today, who are used to the idea of 'Judaism' and 'Christianity' as being two separate religious communities who can coexist harmoniously, but we should be honest about Stephen's argument here (indeed, a similar understanding has emerged in Peter's speeches and continues throughout Acts). It can also be useful to think of a possible Christian version of this argument—a clash between the new and the old, between those parts of the Christian community who value (and are often in control of) key institutions such as churches, synods, councils and educational bodies, and those who want to argue that such institutions are (like the law and the temple) not central to the story.

3 Breaking the boundaries

Acts 8

'A great persecution broke out against the church' (v. 2). This sentence represents a significant breaking of boundaries. 'The church' is really just the word meaning 'the assembly', but 'the assembly' was a word used to refer to the people of Israel (for example, in Leviticus 19:2). In keeping with Stephen's speech, the believers are now 'the assembly'. The persecution reinforces this sense: the believers are now separate from the wider community and in some sense are a threat to it (if there is no threat, why the persecution?).

It is intriguing to wonder why the apostles are safe in Jerusalem while the rest of the believers are not. Perhaps they are too well known and respected (5:25–26), or perhaps 'the apostles' here means (following the logic of chapter 6) one part of the community as opposed to the part represented by Stephen. If so, are the apostles watering down the message to remain in favour? Is Stephen's group unnecessarily confrontational and only has itself to blame? Do the two approaches each have their purpose with respect to a particular 'target audience'? If so, can they remain united despite their differences?

The two incidents that follow both involve Philip, another of the 'seven' who, like Stephen, seems to have a ministry far wider than that suggested in 6:1–6. Philip speaks to the Samaritans and to the eunuch, both of whom could be classed as 'half-Jews'. The history of the relationship between Jews and Samaritans is complex, stretching back to the destruction of the northern kingdom of Israel in 721BC and through to more conflicts and religious competition (the Samaritans had their own rival temple and their own version of the scriptures). Nevertheless, they were clearly 'Jewish' in a way, connected to the same history and yet not 'part of the family'. The eunuch is an outsider in a different way. He is clearly a worshipper of the Jewish God, yet Deuteronomy 23:1 explicitly excluded eunuchs from the 'assembly' of Israel. Both Samaritans and eunuchs now seem to be acceptable. The boundaries of this new 'assembly' are broad, including even these 'half-Jews' (continuing perhaps the logic of Jesus' welcome to the 'outcasts' and 'sinners' within Israel).

It is probably no coincidence that it is the more recent and perhaps more marginal believers ('Greeks' such as Stephen and Philip) who push the boundaries. Here, though, through the actions of Peter and John coming to Samaria, there is a sense of the community holding together, the 'establishment' supporting and encouraging the new developments. Throughout both stories, the Spirit is manifestly at work: God is behind these new developments.

4 The calling of Saul

Acts 9:1–31

Saul's meeting with Jesus on the road is described three times in Acts (here, 22:3–16 and 26:4–18) with minor differences. Saul's own version of the event is found in Galatians 1:13–17. Jesus may be absent but he is continuing to work. It is, in effect, another unintended consequence of the persecution. The scattering of the believers led to the expansion of the community and brought Saul to the Damascus road.

The vision raises three important points. First and most simply, Jesus has been raised by God—Saul is wrong, the believers right—and therefore God supports the version of the Jewish story advocated by Jesus and his disciples. Presumably Saul already knew the disciples' message because of his role in the persecution. The vision simply proved to him that it was right. Second, the words 'I am Jesus, whom you are persecuting' (v. 6) are intriguing. Perhaps it just means 'whose name and teaching you are opposing' but it probably suggests more. Jesus is in some way present in his followers and, thus, when persecuting them, Saul has been persecuting him. Third, Saul's commission to go to the Gentiles is explosive. Here (v. 15) it is communicated to Ananias; in 22:17–22 it was received by Saul a little later in Jerusalem; in 26:16–17 it is spoken directly to Saul by Jesus on the road (which is also the implication in Galatians 1:15–16). Perhaps the meaning of the calling became clear over a period of time. Interestingly, here Saul does not 'hear' his own calling; he receives it (also) through the existing church. However it was received, though, it was explosive. 'Half-

Jews' (ch. 8) might be one thing, as might be Jews who have been scattered to the ends of the earth (2:1–11), but Gentiles are a completely different matter. Many of our churches 'reach out' but to a fringe surrounding them; this is a movement to those completely outside, with no connection or background in the faith at all.

The chapter finishes with a picture of Saul preaching powerfully in the synagogues, but creating serious opposition—which is a foretaste of the rest of the book. In a sense, Saul takes up the mantle of Stephen, whose death he had approved not long before. Verse 31 echoes 5:42 but, led by the Spirit and driven by difficulties within the community and pressure from outside, a crucial transition has taken place. A Jerusalem faith, focused on the twelve apostles, has become a movement spreading far more widely, with new leaders emerging.

5 Peter's travels

Acts 9:32—10:23a

The stories about Aeneas and Tabitha illustrate the continued development of the Church. As in chapter 3, we see the role of miracles in the spread of the Church—the miracle creating the public interest and conviction that God was at work. Most of us do not see miracles of the same nature in our churches today, but it's worth asking what happens in and through the Church that is newsworthy and provokes people to question if God is at work. The miracles have similarities with Jesus': the same Jesus is at work through Peter.

The mention that Peter was staying with 'a tanner' (9:43) sets the scene for the next chapter, for tanners were unclean and thus on the margins of Jewish society. If Peter is staying there, he must not be too scrupulous regarding ritual purity (perhaps the fact that he was there gave Cornelius the courage to invite him to his own home: 10:6). But Peter is about to be taken much further. The boundaries that have been extended are about to be smashed.

Cornelius is depicted as a spiritual man but he clearly has no place within the Jewish community (10:1–2). He is a Gentile, a foreign Italian, and an officer of the oppressive imperial power—an outsider, however pious and sympathetic. It is interesting to consider how we relate to those who are spiritual, pious and seeking to follow God, but are equally outside the Church. Cornelius and Peter receive complementary visions, just as Paul and Ananias did. These major developments are not driven by a single person alone.

Peter's vision is intriguing. The basic point is clear—Peter should not shun 'unclean' food—and shocking, since the distinction between clean and unclean food was established in the law (Leviticus 11; 20:25; Deuteronomy 14:3–20). Jesus' teaching, his death and resurrection, the redefinition of the community and the extension of it to 'half-Jews' had not involved such a direct and blatant overturning of the law. There are two further points, though. First, taken precisely, the voice does not say that there is no distinction between clean and unclean but that God can make the unclean clean (10:15). The distinction in the Jewish law is a starting point, but nothing is impossible for God. Second, the vision is about food, while what follows is about people. Presumably the food is just a way of visualising and talking about the broad concepts of clean and unclean, with the interpretation that 'just as God can make unclean food clean, so he can make unclean Gentiles into his people'. One could take it more narrowly, though: this vision was to encourage Peter to accept the invitation to enter Cornelius' house and mix with him; it was the gift of the Spirit (not this vision by itself) that demonstrated that God had accepted Cornelius (perhaps suggested by 10:28, 44–48).

6 The conversion of Cornelius

Acts 10:23b—11:18

The story of the conversion of Cornelius is so important that it is told twice and in great detail. First Peter explains that 'God has shown me that I should not call anyone impure or unclean' (10:28), which he then develops to the startling conclusion, 'I now realize how true it is that God does not show favouritism but accepts those from every nation who fear him and do what is right' (vv. 34–35). This may seem an un-remarkable statement to us, although often enough in Christian history people have claimed that their nation has God's special favour and the 'whiteness' of the Church of England is still striking. However, within a Jewish framework it was a significant statement. The belief that God had chosen Israel to be his special people was a foundational belief (Exodus 19:5–6), even if it was acknowledged that God's choice was not because of Israel's merit (Deuteronomy 7:6–8). What could it mean for Judaism if the idea of Israel being a favoured, chosen nation was abandoned?

Interestingly, the message that Peter then preaches (vv. 34–43) is very similar to what was preached in Jerusalem in chapters 2—5. Peter has been 'set up' to preach the 'good news of peace' (v. 36)—God has acted to overcome the boundaries—but the message is the same. But what would Peter have done then? Had he already understood enough to have baptized Cornelius and his family? Who knows? Leaving nothing open to interpretation, God, through the gift of the Spirit, visibly demonstrated his acceptance of Cornelius and his family. What else could the church do but give its welcome too (vv. 44–48)? Otherwise, in the words of Gameliel, it might find itself opposing God (5:39).

The repetition of the story in 11:1–17 reinforces the same message. The final sentence is a tremendous conclusion: the Jewish believers in Jerusalem have recognized that the good news about Jesus, bringing forgiveness of sins, can be accepted by Gentiles as well. However, hidden underneath this positive statement are two unresolved issues. First, the very issue for which they criticized Peter has not been resolved. The Gentiles might be given repentance that leads to life but what of the Jewish food laws? Presumably, once a Gentile like Cornelius has entered the community, he should then follow the rules. Second, how energetically is this welcoming of Gentiles to be pursued? Is this case exceptional?

Guidelines

Here are some more issues to ponder. Read through them and ask God to guide you to two or three that you should think and pray about.

- What differences exist within your church community? Are there sections of it that feel marginalized? How can this be addressed?
- How does your church community take care of the weak and vulnerable?
- What institutions or practices are particularly close to your heart? How central should they be to your faith and life? What are the good and bad sides of your love for them?

- If you received persecution and others avoided it, how would you react? How easy would it be to accept that God may be calling you to different roles? Have you experienced anything like this, when you've wondered why others have it easier than you?
- Is there something that you feel God has called you to?
- What boundaries define who is made welcome in your church community?
- Think about your outreach and that of your church community. Is it just to a fringe or to those completely outside? What barriers are there to those outside? What difficulties would it cause for you and your church community if 'real outsiders' wanted to join?

1 The church in Antioch

Acts 11:19–30

Once again we are pointed to the positive outcome of the persecution (see 8:4–5; 9:1–2). Some persecuted Christians do indeed point to positive effects, from Tertullian, the bishop of Carthage in Tunisia in AD197 ('the blood of the martyrs is the seed of the church') to some contemporary Chinese church leaders. However, Christianity in Tunisia was all but wiped out by the Arab conquests and subsequent Islamic rule and the church in countries such as Albania or Russia was severely negatively affected by the communist persecutions. It's a complex issue. Nevertheless, it strengthens the sense that bad things can be used by God—a crucial principle when preaching that Jesus was both God's chosen one and was crucified (Luke 24:17–27; Acts 2:22–24; see also Genesis 50:20; Romans 8:28).

In this passage we also see the continuing development of the believers' community with a two-way relationship between Jerusalem and Antioch. Jerusalem continues to exercise some form of oversight (sending Barnabas, v. 22) and is a spiritual resource (the base of the prophets, v. 27). Antioch offers material support in return (v. 29). It is all too easy for relationships between individuals or churches to be one-way and, hence, hierarchical or patronizing, despite good intentions of 'offering support'. Note also the significance of the disciples being first called 'Christians' (v. 26). This seems to imply that they were now being seen as a separate group from Jews, an inevitable development if non-Jews are joining the community (vv. 19–20) but nevertheless a significant one.

It is not clear what Saul has been doing in Tarsus (he went there in 9:30 to escape threats to his life in Jerusalem). However, Barnabas recognizes that now is the moment for Saul's particular gifts and calling (vv. 25–26). Recognizing the time to bring in someone else is always difficult; soon Saul will outshine Barnabas.

2 Peter and Herod

Acts 12

Immediately we are struck by the reality of persecution. James, one of Jesus' closest disciples (Luke 8:51; 9:28), is murdered by Herod. The timing (during the Passover, vv. 2–4) immediately creates connections with Jesus' own death, in which another Herod (the uncle of the Herod here) was involved (Luke 23:6–12). Even Jesus himself was not saved by God from being killed, nor was James, so what hope is there for Peter? Indeed, neither Peter nor the people meeting in Mary's house seem to have had a particularly strong expectation that God would rescue him, for even Peter interprets what is happening to him as merely 'a vision' (v. 9). Since 'angel' means 'messenger', 'Peter's angel' (v. 15) presumably suggests that the other disciples thought they were to receive a divinely transmitted message from Peter, perhaps similar to the Macedonian in 16:9–10. Although God had rescued Peter from jail before (5:19), that was ten years previously and the current situation seems far more serious. The passage ends with Peter fleeing. Despite the miraculous escape, Acts is not a story of everything going right, of constant rescue and victory for the believers.

The fact that James died and Peter was rescued raises complex questions about God's purposes and prayer. Why did God not save both? The church is said to have been praying 'earnestly' for Peter (vv. 5, 12) but presumably it also prayed in James' case. God did not save Jesus from death, so it was James, not Peter, who most closely copied Jesus' example. We have to conclude that God rescued Peter but not James because of his own purposes: there is no mechanical connection between prayer or faith and God's actions.

This conclusion invites the response, 'Well, then, what is the point of praying?' Many people doubt the appropriateness of praying for specific things because of a similar argument: surely God wants the good anyway; it is terrible if God acts if you pray and not if you don't. Such questions are impossible to answer but the biblical imperative to pray is clear (Luke 18:1–6; Romans 12:12; Ephesians 6:18, Philippians 4:6; Colossians 4:2–4). We should also recognize our innate desire to reduce God to a 'mechanism', a tool, with ourselves at the centre. The idea of God acting or not acting in accordance with his own purposes, which are unknown to us, is deeply unsettling. The human desire to know and to control (that is, to be like God, knowing good and evil: Genesis 3:5) is very strong.

Herod dies as the result of his arrogance (v. 23), but Peter still has to flee to safety elsewhere. James, Jesus' brother, is able to stay in Jerusalem; James, John's brother, is dead. 'But the word of God continued to increase and spread' (v. 24).

3 Barnabas and Saul sent off

Acts 13:1–12

The church in Antioch was truly cosmopolitan and had pioneered preaching to the Gentiles (11:20–23) with Saul's involvement. This built on Peter's experience with Cornelius (10:1—11:18) and had been accepted by the wider Church. Now the scene is set for the next phase.

The words 'for the work to which I have called them' (v. 2) point us back to Ananias' vision about Saul (9:15): he is to be an instrument to bring God's name before Gentiles. However, what we then see is repeated throughout most of Acts: Saul in fact goes to speak to Jewish communities in the 'diaspora' (the 'scattering' of Jews outside Israel), while also speaking to Gentiles along the way. This highlights a peculiarity about Saul. He is said to be the 'apostle to the Gentiles' (Galatians 1:16; 2:8), yet he seems to have preached first to Jews in each place he visited. Perhaps this was down to a theological principle (see Romans 1:16) or perhaps it was a practical matter—his fellow Jews providing a natural 'home base' in a new city. Either way, although he is rightly famous for preaching to the

Gentiles, his life and work were more complex than that. It is easy to turn leaders or the famous into one-dimensional characters.

In this passage we see the name Paul replacing Saul, and Paul's emerging prominence over Barnabas. This was not an actual change of name, for it was common practice to have a Jewish name (Saul) and a Roman name (Paul) (compare John Mark in Acts 12:12). Nevertheless, it is notable that from this point on he is always called Paul. Similarly, until now Barnabas has always been mentioned first. From the incident with Bar-Jesus onwards, however, Paul takes the lead and is always mentioned first. When they arrive in Pisidian Antioch it is Paul, not Barnabas (the 'son of encouragement', 4:36), who is asked to give a word of encouragement (v. 15). This signals a change of focus: for the rest of the book, Paul and his mission to the Gentiles are central. Perhaps it was on this mission that Paul's unique calling became clear.

Barnabas' role is interesting. He was Paul's first contact and sponsor in the Jerusalem church (9:26–27); he realized that Paul's expertise and calling could be used in Antioch, went and found him, brought him to Antioch and worked alongside him (11:25–26). He took Paul with him on the trip to his homeland of Cyprus (v. 4; see 4:36). Then he was overshadowed by Paul and eventually they disagreed sharply and Paul went his own more famous way (15:36–41). To encourage and support others to the point where we are eclipsed by them is a difficult calling (in John the Baptist's words, 'He must become greater; I must become less, John 3:30).

4 Pisidian Antioch

Acts 13:13–52

Acts gives us two main evangelistic speeches of Paul—here to a Jewish audience, later to a Gentile audience (in Athens, 17:22–31, a speech similar to the short one in 14:15–17). The speeches to Jews, whether by Paul, Stephen or Peter, are quite similar, while those to Gentiles are different: the good news is presented differently to different audiences.

Paul presents Jesus as the culmination of Jewish history, which is a history of God's choice and action. God chose their forefathers. He made them prosper, rescued them from Egypt and bore with them in the desert. He overthrew the Canaanites. He gave the Jews the land, the judges, the kings Saul and David. Finally, as promised, he has sent them Jesus. Jesus is fully in keeping with Jewish history and scriptures: he was killed because those in Jerusalem did not understand their own scriptures. Jesus is the fulfilment of God's promises. The scriptures bear witness to this, as did John the Baptist (vv. 24–25). Most importantly, God also bore witness by raising him from the dead. Paul's listeners now need to make a choice. Are they going to accept the message or reject God's message and join the 'scoffers' (vv. 38–41, 46)? Up to now, as Jews, they have been the recipients of God's grace, but in order to continue in the grace of God they must embrace what God has done (v. 43).

Sadly, after a positive initial response, it all goes wrong. It would miss the point to suggest that the Jews were 'jealous' because Paul and Barnabas were drawing large crowds (v. 45). 'Jealous' should really be translated 'zealous', which is the word Paul uses to describe himself before his meeting with Jesus (Galatians 1:14; compare Romans 10:2). It points to their zeal for preserving their identity as the chosen people. If Paul speaks the same message of forgiveness to the whole city, then Jewish identity will be lost (indeed, Paul says that the law of Moses was not sufficient for justification, v. 39). They will become just the same as the Gentiles in the city.

The result is a tragic reversal. The Jews, zealous for their own identity and anxious not to be overwhelmed by the Gentiles, reject God's message while Gentiles accept it. Jews shook the dust off their feet when leaving Gentile lands; now Paul and Barnabas shake the dust off their feet against the Jews, but God's Spirit fills the Gentiles (vv. 50–51; compare Luke 9:5–6; 10:8–11). It's a tragic story but one that is easy to repeat: so keen are we to hold on to our identity and traditions, we reject God's desire to bring his grace and forgiveness to new people, because it might mean that our way of doing things has to change.

5 Iconium, Lystra and Derbe

Acts 14

Iconium is similar to Pisidian Antioch, in that eventually Paul and Barnabas are driven out of town due to the opposition of certain Jews who don't accept their message. However, it is a more positive picture, for in

Iconium a great number of Jews do believe (v. 1). It is easy to presume that Acts works according to stereotypes—Paul preaches in the Jewish synagogues, is rejected, and then turns to the Gentiles—but in fact there is far more difference between the different places. Our church culture today also loves to identify patterns and programmes: 'If you do *x*, then *y* will result; a growing church will be like *z*.' Reality is often more varied and complex.

In Lystra we see a very different situation. Here, there seems to be no Jewish community to act as the starting point of the mission. The miracle creates interest in what Paul and Barnabas are saying (note that what we do determines whether or not people will listen to what we say), but then it all goes wrong. Even if, as foreigners, Paul and Barnabas did not follow the Greek gods Zeus and Hermes, most Mediterranean people were content with a form of syncretism, identifying their own gods with those of other cultures (the Egyptian god Amen-Ra could be seen as 'the same' as the Greek Zeus or Roman Jupiter). They could easily accept that in new places there were local gods who should be honoured, but Jews were different. What happens in Lystra shows that, compared to the wider Gentile world, Paul and Barnabas are fundamentally Jewish: the history they claim is Jewish and their basic beliefs and forms of worship are Jewish. The fact that it is other Jews from Pisidian Antioch and Iconium who, in the end, come and create difficulties only highlights the tragedy. We can often see the same in our world, where conflict between those who share so much can be the most painful and vindictive—conflict within families, within churches or between different understandings of the Church.

Syncretism is a complex issue. While resisting syncretism in one way, Paul tries to establish common ground by presenting God not as a particularly Jewish God but as the creator (v. 15). We see this approach developed further in Athens (17:22–31). The dividing line between syncretism (bringing alien elements into the religion) and finding common ground to aid communication is often blurred. In our own world, what one Christian calls 'selling out', another sees as 'reaching the people in our generation'.

After the conversion of Cornelius, the church concluded that 'God has given even to the Gentiles the repentance that leads to life' (11:18, NRSV). Now the issue has been taken much further and large numbers of Gentiles are believing: God has 'opened the door of faith to the Gentiles' (14:27). Trouble is about to break out.

6 The Council of Jerusalem

It is easy to misunderstand the problem that the 'certain individuals' (v. 1, NRSV) and the believers who were Pharisees (v. 5) had. There is no suggestion that the Gentiles really could not be saved and added to the community of believers in Jesus. There is no going back on the principles already established (11:18, 20–25; 14:26). The point is more subtle.

The suggestion is that Gentiles who come into the community through belief in Jesus should then also take on Jewish practices. God in his mercy is now enlarging his people Israel by adding to it those from outside. Such people (Gentiles) are welcome but, once they are added, surely they should follow the rules of behaviour that God has laid down for his people. Peter rejects this suggestion, arguing that God makes 'no distinction' (v. 9; see 10:34) between those who believe in Jesus, whether they are Jews or Gentiles. The law has not saved Jews, so why put it on Gentiles? All will be saved in the same way, through Jesus (compare Paul in Romans 3:20–22; 10:12–13). James finds scripture which demonstrates that this is not a new idea but was always part of God's plan, and agrees with Peter. The law (and Jewish practices in general) would be an unnecessary burden for the Gentiles: they should be part of the community of believers while remaining Gentiles. Moses' teaching is available if people are interested, but there is no need for them to impose it (v. 21). This position is adopted (vv. 24–28).

James does suggest some restrictions, however, which are also adopted by the council (vv. 20, 28–29). These can seem like a smuggling back in of 'works', as if belief in Jesus is not sufficient and Gentiles do need certain quasi-Jewish practices, but there is probably a more practical reason. The council is effectively creating mixed Jewish-Gentile churches. The people will be united in their belief in Jesus but some will follow Jewish practices and some will not. This sounds fine until one looks at it practically. What type of food will the church eat at their common meals? If the Gentiles don't follow Jewish practices, the Jewish believers will either be (from their point of view) polluted by contact with them or be forced to separate themselves (as we see happening in Galatians 2:11–14). The answer is a set of guide-lines to stop the Gentiles doing things that will particularly offend their Jewish fellow believers and create discord within the community.

The principle presented is challenging. The newcomers to the church should not have to adopt its existing cultural practices, except where this would create significant problems for the functioning of the community. Frequently our churches seem to adopt the approach *defeated* at the council: 'You are welcome to join us, as long as you change to be like us'.

Guidelines

Here is a third list of questions. Identify two or three to pray about.

- Are there people that you or your church community support? Is that relationship two-way? What difference would it make if you received as well as gave?
- Do you sometimes wish that God was a tool, responding clearly and directly to your prayers? Is there an area of life where you find it difficult to accept God's purposes?
- Do you believe that if someone is close to God, they will avoid evil and suffering? Even if you don't believe it in your head, do you act as if it is true?
- Can you identify a leader who you think of as one-dimensional? What difference would it make if you related to him or her as a normal, complex human being?
- Is there somebody you should be helping and encouraging? Is there someone whom you have helped and encouraged who is now overshadowing you? How does that make you feel?
- Think about your 'family'—literal family, colleagues, church community or other groups. Are there divisions within them that shouldn't be too serious but are actually painful and vindictive? How can this change?
- Does 'you are welcome to join us, as long as you change to be like us' sum up your church community's approach to outsiders? What would it mean if people in the wider community joined your church and didn't change to do things just the way you do? Think of some of the members of the wider community who are most distant from your church culture (whether by wealth, age, class, ethnicity or gender). Would they be welcome? Would you cope?

The BRF

Magazine

Richard Fisher writes...

Discipleship was never meant to be a lonely affair. At BRF, we understand the importance of partnership in our spiritual journey: we see its benefits in our work every day as people with a variety of skills and giftings come together to further our ministry. We are also constantly aware of the support we receive from those of you who pray regularly for us—thank you!

Many of you will already know that BRF moved premises in August 2007, and a short report on the move (see page 142) gives you a taste of the excitement we all feel about this new stage in the organization's life. We look forward to developing links with local churches and schools here as time goes on.

Before that, in this issue of the *BRF Magazine*, Sharon Durant outlines the advantages of using *Foundations21*, BRF's web-based discipleship resource, along with others in your church. If you haven't already done so, why not start a group that can share insights and encourage one another to learn and develop from this innovative programme?

We've also chosen four books to bring to your attention in this issue. Naomi recommends *Six Men—Encountering God*, a page-turning collection of real-life testimonies. As Naomi mentions, the witness of Christians is key to each story, showing how we can help

people on to the path of discipleship even before they affirm a faith in Jesus. *Seeking Faith, Finding God*, her second recommendation, encourages us to keep asking questions about faith, and would be an ideal book to study together in a small group.

There are also extracts from *The Fourfold Leadership of Jesus*, essential reading for those whose full-time calling is about enabling other people to become better disciples, and *Footsteps to the Feast*, a book of special events tailor-made to help children enjoy the festivals of the church year. Our extract from this book is from the chapter on Trinity—a reminder, if we needed it, that partnership is at the very heart of the Godhead.

Don't go it alone! Let BRF encourage you to find new ways of joining with others in your journey of discipleship.

Richard Fisher, Chief Executive

What's ongoing and what's going on in your church?

Foundations21
THE NEW WAY TO DO DISCIPLESHIP

Sharon Durant

At first glance, there's not much difference between the phrases 'ongoing' and 'going on', but there is a subtle distinction, which you can clearly see if you look through my notes from office meetings. I often report to my colleagues that something is 'ongoing', meaning I should have done it but haven't got round to it yet. But I wouldn't say that the job was 'going on', because that would imply that I had actually done something about it!

Of course, we also use the word 'ongoing' for the routine parts of our lives that happen regularly over a long stretch of time. Conversely, we talk of things that are 'going on' to mean the events and situations that are taking up our immediate attention.

Discipleship is an ongoing aspect of the church's mandate, but is it going on? Is it really happening and connecting with where people are at the moment— or is discipleship being brushed under the carpet as something mundane and routine, something we might look at when we have more time?

> *Discipleship … not just 'ongoing' but really going on*

Thinking of the church where I worship, the regular programme of home groups provides an opportunity for ongoing discipleship week-by-week; but at 10pm, when we wash up the coffee cups and head back out to everyday life, sometimes I tick 'discipleship' off my list and forget about actively pursuing my faith until the next meeting rolls around.

In using *Foundations21* with others in your church, discipleship can be something that is not just 'ongoing' but really going on and bringing the journey of faith into the centre of the church's activity.

As an individual, you can follow

a pathway through *Foundations21*, exploring twelve key aspects of the Christian faith. With much of the content accessed through your computer and the Internet, you can log on and continue your discipleship at home, at work or even on the train if there's a WiFi connection. Each 'waymarker' you pass plots your progress through *Foundations21* and, consequently, a milestone in your journey of faith.

You can easily take a year (or more) on the material found within *Foundations21*, spending a month looking at each of the topics: God the Father, Jesus, the Holy Spirit, the Cross and Resurrection, Church, the Bible, Prayer, Worship, Intimacy with God, Christian Lifestyle, Christian Ministry and Christian Mission.

With four different learning styles, suited to different personalities, you can explore the rich content of *Foundations21* in a way that suits you and complements other members of the group. Some people use the same learning style throughout; others first use the learning style that best suits them, then take different approaches to the material to look at the topic from a fresh perspective.

Foundations21 is an engrossing experience and all the more fulfilling if you can share the excitement of your faith with like-minded people. Each day there are 'daily deliveries' of Bible passages, Psalms, inspirational thoughts and scripture promises. I have found that when something strikes me as profound, it is easy to share that thought with a friend by email or note it in my *Foundations21* journal for further reflection.

In the course of exploring the learning aspect of discipleship, *Foundations21* links to over 7500 thematically similar articles from external websites. This gives individuals the chance to study at their own level, ponder the personal challenges God may be raising in their lives and share those challenges with a mentor or with the group, which provides the support we all need to grow in our faith.

Each person explores a different avenue and takes their own unique path

As a *Foundations21* group, church members draw support from each other—but not just to keep going. A wide range of opinions and insights can be drawn upon as each person explores a different avenue and takes their own unique path through *Foundations21*. The simple question 'What has God been teaching you through *Foundations21*?' can start a whole evening's discussion and prayer as each person shares from their own experience and the way God has been speaking to them.

Each person has a part to play in the church, however small it may seem, and in the wider world. *Foundations21* enables churches to discover each individual's role in mission and ministry, looking at how those roles can be lived out on the local, national and international stage. There are levels of increasing depth for new, growing and mature Christians.

All sorts of people from all walks of life become involved in church *Foundations21* groups, as it meets a need in churches, offering innovative and thoughtful methods for nurturing anyone—from people taking first steps in faith to leaders looking to revitalize and replenish their faith.

Foundations21 uses the booming world of technology to bring together those who might otherwise remain on the fringes of church life. Those who might be unable to participate in church activities because of unsociable working hours have found that they can log on at the time that suits them. People who can't get out and about to church events can meet and chat online or on the phone.

The emphasis *Foundations21* places on both online and personal contact enables people from all walks of life to be included, and it is simple enough for even those technophobes among us to use with ease.

With all this going on, *Foundations21* has a great deal to offer churches. Not only does it offer a platform for spiritual growth but, with readymade group material such as DVD clips, discussion starters and the beginnings of a sermon series (how about spending one month on each of the twelve topics?), it also weaves discipleship into the core fabric of the church.

A number of churches have now opted to take part, running *Foundations21* groups as part of their regular activities. One church leader who has taken up this opportunity remarked:

26 years ago, I became a Christian and was given a foundation of discipleship that has made me eternally grateful. My prayer is that the experience people are being brought into today with Foundations21 will result in the same feeling of thanks and appreciation in many years to come.

Let's make it our aim that ongoing discipleship will be going on in every part of our lives, as the writer of Hebrews exhorts us, 'Let us… spur one another on towards love and good deeds. Let us not give up meeting together' (10:24–25).

To subscribe to Foundations21, please turn to the form on page 157.

Sharon Durant joined the BRF team in 2005 as a member of the marketing team and was part of the BRF Foundations21 pilot group in 2006.

BRF in Abingdon

Lisa Cherrett

At the end of August 2007, Bible Reading Fellowship completed the purchase of new offices in Abingdon, five miles south of Oxford. The new HQ is close to the town centre and provides BRF and its team of 24 staff with much-needed additional space and scope for further growth in the future.

Packing began some weeks before the move, after a thorough clear-out of the old equipment and stationery that accumulates even in the best-organized offices and homes. On 29 and 30 August, 15 The Chambers started to fill up with carefully labelled boxes and furniture. By the next day, desks and shelves had been installed, books and files had found their new places, and computers had been connected.

The office is on three levels. The second floor houses the editorial department, with marketing and customer services below on the first floor. The ground floor provides ample space for a large meeting room, post and stock room, and kitchen.

As a member of the editorial team, working on the top floor, the biggest difference I've noticed between the new offices and the old is the quietness of the new surroundings. The offices BRF leased for seven years in Oxford were next to the A40, the city's ringroad, bombarded with constant traffic noise and the sound of sirens from emergency vehicles travelling to and from the local hospitals. In Abingdon, set apart from the main roads and overlooking a small courtyard car park, the most noticeable outdoor sound is the occasional cooing of a pigeon—much more conducive to concentration.

Bishop Colin Fletcher, BRF's Chairman of Trustees, has commented, 'As trustees we have been delighted to see the many ways in which God has blessed BRF's ministry over the years. This move represents the opening of another new chapter for the organization and we are excited about what lies ahead.' Those of us who work here echo those thoughts as we have quickly settled into BRF's permanent new home.

15 The Chambers, Abingdon

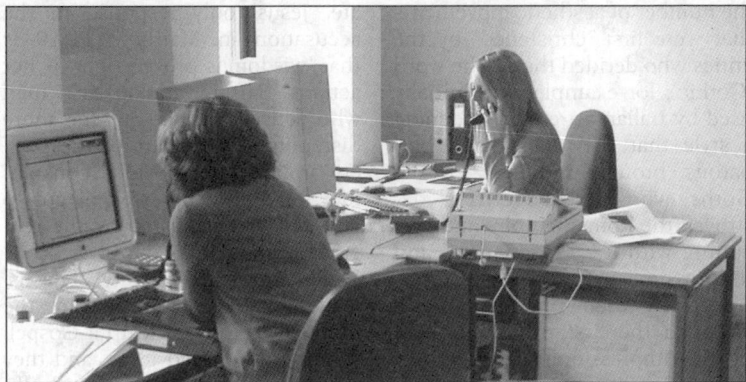

Editorial department, top floor

Lisa Cherrett is BRF's Project Editor and Managing Editor for the Bible reading notes.

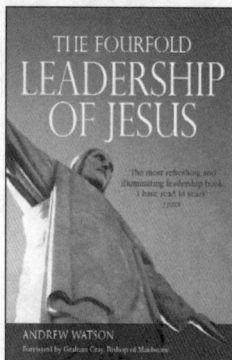

An extract from *The Fourfold Leadership of Jesus*

'Don't follow me. Follow Jesus!' runs a popular slogan, while Paul wrote, 'Follow my example, as I follow the example of Christ.' As leaders, can we ever hope to echo Paul's words—or should we only point away from ourselves to Jesus? In this book, Andrew Watson explores what it means to lead as Jesus led, as he called his disciples to come, to follow, to wait and to go. Those four commands embody the four different aspects of leadership that this book explores as a model for us today. The following extract is an abridged version of Chapter 1, 'Accessible leadership'.

One of the historical oddities referred to in E.H. Gombrich's magnificent book *The Story of Art* is the number of aesthetic movements that were first 'christened' by the critics who derided them. The word 'Gothic', for example, was initially used by Italian art critics to denote a style that they considered barbarous, brought into Italy by the Goths who had effectively destroyed the Roman empire and true culture with it... 'Mannerism' and 'Impressionism' were also terms coined by their opponents, and although the first exhibition held by the Impressionists was widely ridiculed... it wasn't long before Monet and his friends were wearing the Impressionist badge with pride.

The same may be said of the expression 'Friend of tax collectors and sinners'—a term of abuse used by Jesus' opponents but one that Jesus himself never tried to repudiate. Jesus' only response to the accusation in Matthew 11:19 is that 'wisdom is proved right by her actions'. His reputation as a man who actively sought out the more disreputable members of the society around him provided constant fuel for a growing swell of gossip and censure instigated by the religious leaders of his day...

The sheer accessibility of Jesus' leadership is evident from the moment we first pick up a Gospel. 'Come to me,' said Jesus, and they came—synagogue rulers, royal officials, Pharisees and members of the Jewish ruling council; tax collectors, lepers, unspecified 'sinners' and women with unmentionable diseases; parents wanting Jesus to bless their little children and mothers seeking preferment for their big children, as well as… Roman centurions, Samaritans, Canaanites, Greeks and some exotic visitors from the east, bearing gifts of gold, frankincense and myrrh…

Why, then, was he willing to associate with quite such mixed and frequently unsavoury company? Why was he ready to court such hostility for the stand he took on this particular issue? The answer is that accessibility lay at the very heart of the mission to which Jesus knew himself to be called. He was the Son of Man, come to seek and to save the lost. He was the shepherd called to find the sheep that had strayed. He was the doctor whose availability to the sick was integral to his sense of vocation (Luke 19:10; 15:4; Matthew 9:12). In response to his opponents, Jesus would sometimes use the word 'sinner' as they did, but his own preference was to speak the non-pejorative language of lostness and disease. For the shepherd to ignore the sheep who had strayed, or for the doctor to keep his distance from the patients who so desperately needed him, would have been the gravest dereliction of duty, the most basic disregard of the call to pastor and to heal.

There are many reasons, of course, why leaders frequently like to keep their distance. Shyness, privacy, stress, busyness: all play their part in building an invisible barrier between the leader and those who are led, while the question of leadership priorities becomes particularly acute as an organization begins to grow. But practicalities like these were not responsible for the outrage with which Jesus' radical accessibility was greeted. Underlying that anger lay two basic values to which his opponents were variously committed: the cultivation of leadership mystique on the one hand, and the commitment to ritual purity on the other.

Misleadership: mystique and ritual purity

'Mystique' was a concept that the classical world inherited from Persia… As John Adair puts it, it was the Persians who had 'introduced prostration as part of a novel method of creating an aura of divinity around their kings'. This 'aura of divinity' was maintained through the remoteness of the king from his people, and found expression in the increasingly elaborate palaces, courtyards and protective walls that bedecked the ancient world…

Classical culture had a contrary tradition, too, in which a leader made himself accessible to his people… The Greek historian Flavius Arrianus describes how the young Alexander the Great showed deep concern for the wounded after one of the battles in his Persian campaign: 'He visited them all,' writes Arrianus, 'and examined their wounds, asking each man how and in what circumstances his wound was received, and allowing him to tell the story and exaggerate as much as he pleased'! But even Alexander, that exemplary model of motivational leadership, seems to have been progressively seduced by the Persian approach. John Adair charts his growing self-importance in later years, fuelled by flattering courtiers, both Greek and Persian, who puffed up his pretensions to be a living god…

Caesar Augustus, introduced to us at the beginning of Luke's Gospel, had largely bought into the culture of 'mystique': the name 'Augustus' ('exalted') is a simple reminder of that fact. Even the puppet-king Herod Agrippa happily received the adulation of his people ('This is the voice of a god, not of a mere mortal', Acts 12:22) and died five days later in an incident that both Luke and the Jewish historian Josephus regarded as an act of divine retribution. Against this background it is hardly surprising that the accessibility of Jesus did not endear him to his Roman hearers. Jesus' words in Mark 10:42, 'Those who are regarded as rulers of the Gentiles lord it over them, and their high officials exercise authority over them', prove that he would never see eye-to-eye with his Roman contemporaries on leadership issues…

While mystique was part of the Roman world of Jesus' day, the Jewish culture was far more focused on the theme of ritual purity. Taking their lead from the holiness code in the Torah… and amplifying the Torah's regulations with a hundred-and-one fiddly bylaws, the Pharisees were outraged at the laxity of Jesus and the dangers of moral contagion from the company he kept. Simon the Pharisee's response to the embarrassing gatecrasher who wiped the feet of Jesus with ointment and tears is typical of this approach: 'If this man were a prophet, he would know who is touching him and what kind of woman she is—that she is a sinner' (Luke 7:39). The beginning of that sentence—'If this man were a prophet'—suggests that even the more sympathetic of the Pharisees regarded Jesus' radical accessibility as a major stumbling block to their acceptance of his authority as one sent by God.

Jesus' response to such criticism has already been noted, and the 'doctor' image is especially suggestive. Yes, evil can be contagious: it can infect us like yeast 'infects' a batch of dough (see

> *Caesar Augustus had largely bought into the culture of 'mystique'*

Jesus' warning in Matthew 16:6). But goodness—the power of the kingdom to forgive, restore, transform and heal—is more contagious still. Jesus never underestimated the grip of sin in our lives as some more liberal commentators are prone to do: 'everyone who sins is a slave to sin', as he put it bluntly in John 8:34. Yet the Spirit's anointing to 'proclaim freedom for the prisoners and recovery of sight for the blind' (Luke 4:18) most clearly rested upon him, and with it came a completely new approach to holiness, which was proactive, not reactive; faithful, not fearful; on the front foot, not constantly in retreat. The great commission of Matthew 28 would perhaps have been fulfilled by now had only the Church emulated our Lord's example.

> *With it came a completely new approach to holiness*

Jesus the shepherd

In contrast to these misleaders, Jesus' call to 'come to me' took its cue from a deep biblical image: the picture of God as shepherd alongside the 'under-shepherding' of prophet, priest and king. The good shepherd in this image was one who gathered the sheep to himself. The bad shepherd was consistently responsible for their scattering.

Having bad shepherds was tantamount to having no shepherds at all, as the prophet Micaiah was bold enough to remind weak King Ahab. 'I saw all Israel scattered on the hills like sheep without a shepherd', he announced, earning for himself Ahab's grumpy response, 'Didn't I tell you that he never prophesies anything good about me, but only bad?' The context of this story is also instructive, with Ahab having gathered the people to fight the king of Aram. In the absence of a good shepherd-king (one modelled on the life of David), Micaiah warned Ahab that such attempts to gather were inappropriate. Instead Ahab should let the Israelites disperse, scatter…

Moving from (arguably) the worst shepherd in the Old Testament to (unarguably) the best, the most tender example of 'Come to me' leadership appears in a famous passage in Isaiah 40. There it is said of God himself, 'He tends his flock like a shepherd: he gathers the lambs in his arms and carries them close to his heart; he gently leads those that have young' (v. 11)…

In the New Testament, this gathering imagery, in a startlingly feminine form, is a feature of Jesus' leadership in his lament over Jerusalem: 'Jerusalem, Jerusalem… how often I have longed to gather your children together, as a hen gathers her chicks under her wings, but you were not willing' (Matthew 23:37). His image of the good shepherd who 'calls his own sheep by name' (John 10:3) is similarly powerful… And Jesus didn't simply speak in such terms. Time and time again, he practised what he preached, gathering the most unlikely group of people to himself, frequently around a meal table.

The most famous 'Come to me' invitation of them all is also the most illuminating. 'Come to me,' said Jesus, 'all you who are weary and burdened, and I will give you rest. Take my yoke upon you and learn from me, for I am gentle and humble in heart, and you will find rest for your souls. For my yoke is easy and my burden is light' (Matthew 11:28–30).

Of course, many people are weary and burdened, and a hundred Christian generations have rightly found comfort in this warm and winsome invitation. But Jesus may have had a particular type of hearer in mind when he issued it—not simply those who were wearied by life in general but those who were burdened by the incessant demands of the religious leaders, with their intrusive interpretations of the law. As he said later of the Pharisees, 'They tie up heavy, cumbersome loads and put them on other people's shoulders, but they themselves are not willing to lift a finger to move them' (Matthew 23:4).

The 'yoke' of the law was later mentioned in the critical discussions of the Council of Jerusalem. In debating the question of the Church's accessibility to its growing Gentile membership, Peter wisely posed the question, 'Why do you try to test God by putting on the necks of Gentiles a yoke that neither we nor our ancestors have been able to bear?' (Acts 15:10). It's hardly surprising, then, that Jesus' gracious invitation to lay down that burden and replace it with an 'easy' yoke (perhaps in the sense of being fit for use and tailor-made for the wearer) was to prove so attractive.

It might seem ill-advised to seek to rehabilitate a much-derided children's hymn at this point. But the verse, 'Gentle Jesus, meek and mild, look upon a little child' picks up some of the major traits of 'Come to me' leadership rather well, whatever its sentimental associations. Gentleness, meekness, mildness—or, to modernize the words a little, gentleness, humility and a peaceable spirit—join compassion and vulnerability as key qualities in the character of Jesus, and these virtues help to explain the radical accessibility which was to prove such a significant feature of his ministry. It is to these 'come to me' qualities that we now turn.

To order a copy of this book, please turn to the order form on page 159.

The Editor recommends

Naomi Starkey

As we seek to grow in faith, to travel further along the discipleship road, it is important to remember that what encourages and builds up one person may actually have little impact on another, or may even discourage them. Our personalities—the fact that God created us as unique individuals—means that our ways of learning, worshipping and sharing our faith are often very different from those of family, friends and fellow church members.

In producing books and Bible reading notes to resource a wide cross-section of the Church, BRF works to ensure that, as far as possible, such differences are catered for. As we plan our publishing programme, we bear in mind that the theological tome that excites one reader may seem dry as dust to the next person, who prefers to browse a short volume of poetic prayers and meditations. Looking at it another way, it is exciting to help create a resource that interests someone in a part of the Bible they have traditionally considered 'boring'—or provides an accessible introduction to a new way of praying for those who feel quite happy with the way they've always done things, thank you very much.

For many people, hearing about 'how it happened to me' is a powerful way of learning more of how and why God works. *Six Men—Encountering God* is a book of stories shared by six individuals, each of whom, in different ways and at different times, came 'face to face with God'. As a result, their lives were never the same again.

Reading the book, we meet the rock climber facing a certain-to-be-fatal fall, the wheeler-dealer whose fortunes crash disastrously, and the cynic whose prejudices are confounded when the Holy Spirit gets to work. Along with the other men featured, they share a pivotal experience, either a moment of crisis or a process of gradual realization, when they recognize a 'God-shaped gap' within.

Six Men—Encountering God is both a call to continue to seek God ourselves (and give thanks for the relationship with him that we already have) and an inspiration and encouragement to marriage partners, family or church members who are longing for a particular person to come to faith. As each story unfolds, the part played by prayer and faithful, low-key witness is shown time and again to be crucial in nudging somebody towards the kingdom, even if the timescale involved is a long one.

Author Brad Lincoln is now a company director but previously spent five years working in Nepal with his family, where he oversaw the International Nepal Fellowship's work in the western region of the country. He has written his book for those who feel they know God well and want to get better acquainted with how he works in people's lives—but also for those who may doubt that God exists at all. Both the book and its author are warmly endorsed in a foreword by former South African rugby captain François Pienaar, who shares something of his own path to Christian faith.

While this story-based book provides a dramatic way of reflecting on whether or not faith works, *Seeking Faith, Finding God* by John Rackley offers a more measured approach. Subtitled 'Getting to grips with questions of faith', John's book grew out of the popular 'Rackley's Reflections' column that he has contributed to *The Baptist Times* over recent years.

Grouped in five sections (A yearning faith; A gospel place; Gospel encounters; Faith companions; Praying the gospel), the pithy Bible-based reflections are based around a fundamental question: what does it mean to be a disciple of Jesus, living according to his gospel in today's world? John is keen to show the importance of developing a 'seeking and searching' faith if we want to be effective witnesses to what we believe.

The society around us continues to change rapidly, sometimes for the better, often for the worse; we live in 'difficult and demanding times', as John points out. The challenge before us is to find ways of explaining what we know to be true to a world that is not only confident that the Church has little to offer but also profoundly ignorant of God's revelation.

Seeking Faith, Finding God is a book that lends itself to group reading and discussion, and is also commended by Paddy Lane of the Retreat Association. As we read it, we are reminded of the importance of holding on to questions and being honest in our struggle to understand and believe what the Bible tells us. In so doing, we are better able to connect with those outside or on the fringes of the Church. They may yearn to come further in but fear that their faith is insufficient; they need to hear Jesus' gentle words about the size of a mustard seed.

To order either of these books, please turn to the order form on page 159.

An extract from
Footsteps to the Feast

In *Footsteps to the Feast*, Martyn Payne offers the opportunity to explore the 'big story' of God's purpose for his world through twelve fun-filled two-hour special events. Each programme is packed with tried and tested ideas including icebreakers, games, drama, music and crafts, and at the heart of each event there is space for visual storytelling and reflection. The programmes explore the feasts and festivals of Advent, Holy Week, Harvest, Epiphany, Pentecost, Hallowe'en and All Saints, Candlemas, Trinity, St Michael and All Angels, Lent, The early Church and Bible Sunday. The following is an extract from '3–2–1 Go! A special event for the feast of Trinity'.

The feast of Trinity comes on the Sunday immediately after Pentecost and celebrates the mystery of God as three persons in one. Christians describe the fullness of God using the formula 'God the Father, God the Son and God the Holy Spirit'. This understanding of God is drawn from the teachings of the Bible and the life and words of Jesus in particular.

It is not an easy concept for adults, let alone children, to understand, and for many outside the Christian faith it can seem as if Christians are worshipping not one God but three. This is a particular stumbling block to Jews and Muslims, who firmly believe that there is only one God. In fact, Christians believe this too, but they see God in action in three distinct ways: as the creator, the redeemer and the sanctifier. They believe that the hidden face of God the Father was made visible on earth as Jesus, and that the life of God the Son is experienced in Christians as the Holy Spirit, who is the invisible God living inside people.

The Trinity is the Church's attempt to embrace the experience of these three elements of the Godhead, and celebrates this fuller understanding of the true character of God. The feast of Trinity reminds each of us that we owe our existence, our salvation and the possibility of new life and change to this reality. What follows is a two-hour programme to present this truth in some lively and memorable ways using story, games, craft and drama.

❀❀❀

Here is a way of telling the story of the baptism of Jesus with all the children together, inviting them to get involved in some simple drama. For props, you will need a blue sheet, something camel-coloured for John to wear and a simple drape for Jesus. Gather the children in a circle, but with a good clear space in the middle where the action will take place.

Introduce the story by laying across the circle the blue sheet folded into a long, thin strip. Begin the story with the words 'Something strange was happening down by the river. Someone was shouting at the top of his voice.'

Invite someone to play the part of John. This person needs to have a good shouting voice! Teach them this line: 'Change your ways! Get ready for the Lord!'

Practise this several times loudly and, as each new piece of the drama is added, return to the character of John to hear this message shouted again.

Continue with the story by saying, 'All sorts of people heard that something strange was going on down by the river and so they all came to see for themselves.'

You will now need five groups of people (of whatever numbers you can manage, according to the total size of your group). Introduce each of these groups, one at a time, and make sure they each establish their actions and words before the next group is introduced. Don't forget, in between each group, to return to John to hear him shouting his message for everyone. If possible, assign an adult leader to each group to prompt their words and movements.

❁ **Group 1: the soldiers:** This group should march around the circle using the chant 'Left, right; left, right; do what we tell you.'

❁ **Group 2: the tax collectors:** This group should creep around the circle using the chant 'Money from him, money from her; all the more for me.'

❁ **Group 3: ordinary people:** This group should walk around the circle shaking their heads selfishly with the chant 'This is mine and not for you; I'll keep it for myself.'

❁ **Group 4: the Pharisees:** This group should walk tall and proudly around the circle to the chant of 'We're God's chosen; so listen to us.'

❁ **Group 5: the king and his court:** This group should stay in one place and keep their distance from John with the chant 'I'll do what I like, so go take a hike!'

As the story unfolds, introduce the arrival of each group punctuated by the shouting from John. Build this up so that it becomes a real chorus of chants and shouting. Something very strange was going on by the river!

Say, 'John demanded that each group should change their ways.' Ask the children how they think each of the groups could change their ways. What might John have said to them? Perhaps it might have been something like 'Don't bully others', 'Don't be greedy', 'Don't be selfish' and so on. Ask the children to suggest what other things John might have said.

Some of the people did change their ways. To show this, take one or two from each of the groups up to John in turn. They should bow down and be covered by the blue sheet for a short moment—being 'baptized' as a sign that they want to change and be different. John could say the words 'Be baptized and get ready for the Lord.' Some from each of the groups should be 'baptized', but the group around the king do not get involved. You might mention that the king (King Herod) was so angry with what John was saying about him that eventually he arrested John and put him into prison.

While these baptisms were going on, something else very strange happened. John's cousin Jesus appeared (choose someone to play the part of Jesus). Jesus went right up to John, who was standing in the water, and asked John to baptize him. John was shocked because he recognized that Jesus was the 'Lord' he was talking about. John told Jesus that he, John, should be the one to be baptized by Jesus. But Jesus said that, for now, it should be the other way around.

Invite the child chosen to play the part of Jesus to bend down and be covered by the blue sheet of water as he is 'baptized'. Describe to the children what was heard and seen when this happened. There was a voice from heaven ('This is my own dear Son and I am pleased with him') and the Spirit of God in the form of a dove alighted upon Jesus. You could emphasize this with some appropriate actions for the dove and by cupping your hands around your mouth to make a 'microphone' for God's words. The three sides to the character of God were together in one place: Father, Son and Holy Spirit.

Jesus was very special. The people nearby saw his baptism and began to follow Jesus rather than John. John had done his work. At the conclusion of the story, ask the following questions:

- ✪ I wonder how John felt as he baptized his cousin, Jesus?
- ✪ I wonder what the crowds made of the voice and the dove?
- ✪ I wonder what John was thinking as he saw people start to follow Jesus and not him?
- ✪ I wonder if the crowds understood that God was in the voice, in the dove and in Jesus?

To order a copy of this book, please turn to the order form on page 159.

Guidelines © BRF 2008

The Bible Reading Fellowship
15 The Chambers, Vineyard, Abingdon OX14 3FE, United Kingdom
Tel: 01865 319700; Fax: 01865 319701
E-mail: enquiries@brf.org.uk
Website: www.brf.org.uk

ISBN 978 1 84101 476 0

Distributed in Australia by:
Willow Connection, PO Box 288, Brookvale, NSW 2100.
Tel: 02 9948 3957; Fax: 02 9948 8153;
E-mail: info@willowconnection.com.au
Available also from all good Christian bookshops in Australia.
For individual and group subscriptions in Australia:
Mrs Rosemary Morrall, PO Box W35, Wanniassa, ACT 2903.

Distributed in New Zealand by:
Scripture Union Wholesale, PO Box 760, Wellington
Tel: 04 385 0421; Fax: 04 384 3990; E-mail: suwholesale@clear.net.nz

Distributed in Canada by:
The Anglican Book Centre, 80 Hayden Street, Toronto, Ontario, M4Y 3G2
Tel: 001 416 924-1332; Fax: 001 416 924-2760;
E-mail: abc@anglicanbookcentre.com; Website: www.anglicanbookcentre.com

Publications distributed to more than 60 countries

Acknowledgments
The New Revised Standard Version of the Bible, Anglicized Edition, copyright © 1989,
1995 by the Division of Christian Education of the National Council of the Churches
of Christ in the USA. Used by permission. All rights reserved.

The Holy Bible, New International Version, copyright © 1973, 1978, 1984 by
International Bible Society. Used by permission of Hodder & Stoughton Limited. All
rights reserved. 'NIV' is a registered trademark of International Bible Society. UK
trademark number 1448790.

Robert Alter, *Genesis: A Translation with Commentary*, Norton, 2004.

Printed in Singapore by Craft Print International Ltd

BRF is a Christian charity committed to resourcing the spiritual journey of adults and children alike. For adults, BRF publishes Bible reading notes and books and offers an annual programme of quiet days and retreats. Under its children's imprint *Barnabas*, BRF publishes a wide range of books for those working with children under 11 in school, church and home. BRF's *Barnabas Ministry* team offers INSET sessions for primary teachers, training for children's leaders in church, quiet days, and a range of events to enable children themselves to engage with the Bible and its message.

We need your help if we are to make a real impact on the local church and community. In an increasingly secular world people need even more help with their Bible reading, their prayer and their discipleship. We can do something about this, but our resources are limited. With your help, if we all do a little, together we can make a huge difference.

How can you help?

- You could support BRF's ministry with a donation or standing order (using the response form overleaf).

- You could consider making a bequest to BRF in your will, and so give lasting support to our work. (We have a leaflet available with more information about this, which can be requested using the form overleaf.)

- And, most important of all, you could support BRF with your prayers.

Whatever you can do or give, we thank you for your support.

BRF – resourcing your spiritual journey

BRF MINISTRY APPEAL RESPONSE FORM

Name _____

Address _____

_____ Postcode _____

Telephone _____ Email _____

(tick as appropriate)

Gift Aid Declaration

❏ I am a UK taxpayer. I want BRF to treat as Gift Aid Donations all donations I make from 6 April 2000 until I notify you otherwise.

Signature _____ Date _____

❏ I would like to support BRF's ministry with a regular donation by standing order (please complete the Banker's Order below).

Standing Order – Banker's Order

To the Manager, Name of Bank/Building Society _____

Address _____

_____ Postcode _____

Sort Code _____ Account Name _____

Account No _____

Please pay Royal Bank of Scotland plc, Drummonds, 49 Charing Cross, London SW1A 2DX (Sort Code 16-00-38), for the account of BRF A/C No. 00774151

The sum of _____ pounds on ___ /___ /___ (insert date your standing order starts) and thereafter the same amount on the same day of each month until further notice.

Signature _____ Date _____

Single donation

❏ I enclose my cheque/credit card/Switch card details for a donation of
£5 £10 £25 £50 £100 £250 (other) £ _____ to support BRF's ministry

Credit/Switch card no. ☐☐☐☐ ☐☐☐☐ ☐☐☐☐ ☐☐☐☐ ☐☐☐☐ ☐☐☐☐

Expires ☐☐☐☐ Security code ☐☐☐ Issue no. of Switch card ☐☐☐☐

Signature _____ Date _____

(Where appropriate, on receipt of your donation, we will send you a Gift Aid form)

❏ Please send me information about making a bequest to BRF in my will.

Please detach and send this completed form to: Richard Fisher, BRF, 15 The Chambers, Vineyard, Abingdon OX14 3FE. BRF is a Registered Charity (No.233280)

GL0208

FOUNDATIONS21 SUBSCRIPTION

Name _____

Address _____

_____ Postcode _____

Telephone _____ Email _____

	Quantity	Price	Total
Foundations21 45-day trial membership pack	_____	£7.99	_____

Includes a DVD of video clips for Room 1 (Jesus),
Disciple Master DVD Room 1 (Jesus),
unlimited online membership for 45 days.

	Quantity	Price	Total
Foundations21 annual subscription	_____	£59.00	_____

Includes a DVD of video clips for Rooms 1-12,
Disciple Master DVD Rooms 1-12 and unlimited
online membership for a year.

To be able to use Foundations21 you will need the following minimum
system requirements on your computer: Pentium III - 500 Mhz processor,
64MB RAM (128 or higher recommended), Audio capability, Windows
98SE/XP, Internet Explorer 6, DVD-ROM drive, Internet connection
(preferably broadband).

You will also need: Java™ Virtual Machine for Windows®, Microsoft®
Windows® Media Player, Macromedia® Flash® Player for Windows®.
These are already installed on many computers or can be downloaded FREE
from the Internet.

Total enclosed £ _____(cheques should be made payable to 'BRF')

Payment by cheque ❏ postal order ❏ Visa ❏ Mastercard ❏ Switch ❏

Credit/Switch card no. ⬜⬜⬜⬜⬜⬜⬜⬜⬜⬜⬜⬜⬜⬜⬜⬜⬜⬜⬜⬜

Expires ⬜⬜⬜⬜ Security code ⬜⬜⬜ Issue no. of Switch card ⬜⬜⬜⬜

Signature (essential if paying by credit/Switch card)_____

*Foundations21 is available by monthly payments and at special rates
for groups. Visit www.foundations21.org.uk*

BRF, 15 The Chambers, Vineyard, Abingdon OX14 3FE. BRF is a Registered Charity

SUBSCRIPTIONS

❏ Please send me a Bible reading resources pack to encourage Bible reading in my church
❏ I would like to take out a subscription myself (complete your name and address details only once)
❏ I would like to give a gift subscription (please complete both name and address sections below)

Your name _____

Your address _____

_____Postcode _____

Gift subscription name _____

Gift subscription address _____

_____Postcode _____

Please send *Guidelines* beginning with the September 2008 / January / May 2009 issue: (delete as applicable)

(please tick box)	UK	SURFACE	AIR MAIL
GUIDELINES	❏ £13.35	❏ £14.55	❏ £16.65
GUIDELINES 3-year sub	❏ £30.00		

I would like to take out an annual subscription to *Quiet Spaces* beginning with the next available issue:

(please tick box)	UK	SURFACE	AIR MAIL
QUIET SPACES	❏ £16.95	❏ £18.45	❏ £20.85

Please complete the payment details below and send your coupon, with appropriate payment, to:
BRF, 15 The Chambers, Vineyard, Abingdon OX14 3FE.

Total enclosed £ _____ (cheques should be made payable to 'BRF')

Payment by cheque ❏ postal order ❏ Visa ❏ Mastercard ❏ Switch ❏

Card number: ☐☐☐☐☐☐☐☐☐☐☐☐☐☐☐☐☐☐

Expires: ☐☐☐☐ Security code ☐☐☐ Issue no (Switch): ☐☐☐☐

Signature (essential if paying by credit/Switch card) _____

BRF is a Registered Charity

BRF PUBLICATIONS ORDER FORM

Please ensure that you complete and send off both sides of this order form.

Please send me the following book(s):

		Quantity	Price	Total
581 1	The Path of Celtic Prayer (C. Miller)	____	£6.99	____
545 3	The Starship Discovery Holiday Club (J. Hardwick)	____	£8.99	____
435 7	The Fourfold Leadership of Jesus (A. Watson)	____	£7.99	____
528 6	Six Men—Encountering God (B. Lincoln)	____	£7.99	____
543 9	Seeking Faith—Finding God (J. Rackley)	____	£6.99	____
464 7	Footsteps to the Feast (M. Payne)	____	£8.99	____
314 5	PBC: Genesis (G. West)	____	£8.99	____
095 3	PBC: Joshua & Judges (S.D. Mathewson)	____	£7.99	____
242 1	PBC: Ruth, Esther, Ecclesiastes, Song, Lamentations (R. Fyall)	____	£8.99	____
118 9	PBC: 1 & 2 Kings (S.B. Dawes)	____	£7.99	____
040 3	PBC: Ezekiel (E. Lucas)	____	£7.99	____
191 2	PBC: Matthew (J. Proctor)	____	£8.99	____
029 8	PBC: John (R.A. Burridge)	____	£8.99	____
216 2	PBC: Acts (L. Alexander)	____	£8.99	____
536 9	PBC: 1 Corinthians (J. Murphy-O'Connor)	____	£7.99	____
119 6	PBC: Timothy, Titus and Hebrews (D. France)	____	£7.99	____

POSTAGE AND PACKING CHARGES

order value	UK	Europe	Surface	Air Mail
£7.00 & under	£1.25	£3.00	£3.50	£5.50
£7.01–£30.00	£2.25	£5.50	£6.50	£10.00
Over £30.00	free	prices on request		

Total cost of books £ _____

Donation £ _____

Postage and packing £ _____

TOTAL £ _____

See over for payment details. All prices are correct at time of going to press, are subject to the prevailing rate of VAT and may be subject to change without prior warning.

PAYMENT DETAILS

Please complete the payment details below and send with appropriate payment and completed order form to:

**BRF, 15 The Chambers, Vineyard,
Abingdon OX14 3FE**

Name _____

Address _____

_____

_____ Postcode _____

Telephone _____

Email _____

Total enclosed £ _____(cheques should be made payable to 'BRF')

Payment by cheque ❑ postal order ❑ Visa ❑ Mastercard ❑ Switch ❑

Card number: ⬚⬚⬚⬚⬚⬚⬚⬚⬚⬚⬚⬚⬚⬚⬚⬚⬚⬚⬚⬚⬚⬚⬚

Expires: ⬚⬚⬚⬚ Security code ⬚⬚⬚ Issue no (Switch): ⬚⬚⬚⬚

Signature (essential if paying by credit/Switch card)_____

❑ Please do not send me further information about BRF publications.

ALTERNATIVE WAYS TO ORDER

Christian bookshops: All good Christian bookshops stock BRF publications. For your nearest stockist, please contact BRF.

Telephone: The BRF office is open between 09.15 and 17.30.
To place your order, phone 01865 319700; fax 01865 319701.

Web: Visit www.brf.org.uk

GL0208